A HOLY PURSUIT

A HOLY PURSUIT

HOW *the* GOSPEL FREES US *to* FOLLOW *and* LAY DOWN OUR DREAMS

DIANNE JAGO

Printed in the United States of America

978-1-5359-6235-3

Published by B&H Publishing Group
Nashville, Tennessee

Dewey Decimal Classification: 153.2
Subject Heading: GOALS (PSYCHOLOGY) / DECISION MAKING / DESIRE

Cover design by Matt Lehman. Imagery © OctopusArtis/creativemarket; ESB Professional/shutterstock. Author photo by Kaiden Jago.

1 2 3 4 5 6 7 • 24 23 22 21 20

To my husband, Ethan,
who faithfully models loving Jesus with all
his heart, soul, mind, and strength.

ACKNOWLEDGMENTS

First and foremost, thanks to my Lord and Savior Jesus Christ. Thank You for pursuing me, drawing me to You, and saving me from the path of destruction I was on. May the words on these pages honor and glorify You alone.

Second, there are not enough pages in this book to thank the many people whose influence and discipleship on my own life have shaped so many of the ideas in this book.

Thanks to my incredible husband, Ethan. Not only have you given me so much freedom and support with all my crazy endeavors, more important, you love and lead me well. So much of this book is the result of your loving guidance and wisdom.

Thanks to my beautiful children, Kaiden, Skye, and Cora. I am beyond blessed to be your mama. I am grateful for the ways God has used you to sanctify me as we journey this life together.

Thanks to my mom and dad, Dale and Irene Stewart, who raised me in a loving, Christian home. Mom and Dad, though I did not always appreciate your love, discipline, and direction growing up, as an adult I cannot thank you enough for always pointing me to the upright, God-honoring path. Time and time again you've modeled for me what it is to be patient, offer forgiveness, and extend grace.

Thank you to my in-laws, Glenn and Tammy Jago, who have become a second set of parents to me. Dad, your knowledge of and love for Scripture, and Mom, your consistent encouragement to prioritize my first callings ("Keep the main thing, the main thing!") have had a profound impact on my walk with God.

Thank you to the many faithful, Bible-preaching churches we've had the privilege to serve in: All Nations Bible Church (Milwaukee, Wisconsin), Parkway Community Church (Fairfield, California), CrossPointe Church (Columbus, Georgia), Lebanon Evangelical Free (Lebanon, Pennsylvania), Church of the Open Door (Fort Washington, Pennsylvania), and Olive Baptist Church (Pensacola, Florida).

Thank you to the many teachers, mentors, friends, and family members who consistently point me to Jesus. There are truly too many to name but each one of you has spoken into my life in ways I will never forget.

Thank you to our faithful *Deeply Rooted Magazine* readers and customers, whose prayers, words of encouragement, and support sustain us issue to issue. Since day one, you've believed in our dream and our mission. Thank you to the Deeply Rooted Team—past, present, and future. I couldn't do this without you. This book is as much a story about you as it is me.

Thank you to B&H Publishing for believing in the words of this book enough to publish them. Thank you for your mission and for this incredible opportunity. Thank you to my wonderful editor, Ashley Gorman, who deserves much credit for her God-given talent of shaping ideas and wrangling in my thoughts. And thank you to Mary Wiley, Jenaye White, Devin Maddox, and the countless others who have contributed so much to the making of this book.

Lastly, thank you to every reader who holds this book in their hands now. Your support means the world to me.

I don't think we will ever know the exponential reach and true ripple effect that a life lived for the glory of God has on other people. There are many names I didn't name but the Lord knows who they are. These people and so many more, though called to different seasons of life and serving in different capacities, all pursue the same end goal which is glorifying their great God.

CONTENTS

INTRODUCTION

We don't have to look far to find a book, inspirational quote, or Instagram post telling us to chase after our dreams. Whether written by a hopeful atheist or an evangelical Christian, we find these messages everywhere:

> *If your dream doesn't scare you, you're not dreaming big enough.*
>
> *Never give up on something you can't go a day without thinking about.*
>
> *The cost of not following your heart is spending the rest of your life wishing you had.*
>
> *#hustle #goals #dowhatyoulove #girlboss #followyourdreams*

Women across the world are bombarded with messages like these. When scroll after scroll after scroll on our newsfeed is filled with seemingly perfect women *doing all the things*, it's no surprise that we experience growing discontent, wondering if we too should be chasing after our dreams.

These mantras and those like it not only overlook the Christian's primary aim in life—to live for God's glory alone—but they seep into Christian culture, adopt a Christian twist, and disguise themselves as wisdom. Within many church circles, we are told that "true freedom" and huge impact on the kingdom of God come from unlocking His "purpose" in our lives—as if more is required beyond the call to love

Him and our neighbors. We are assured that because "God is for us," He is certainly for our dreams too, without any consideration for the correct meaning and original context of the passages we build our dreams upon. And so, we chase wildly after our dream because if we have a deep longing, God must want us to pursue it. We tie our identities to God plus the dream itself, and our forward-focused wishing, hoping, and hustling inevitably result in comparison, dissatisfaction, and exhaustion.

What happens when our dreams don't turn out as expected? We might be left feeling purposeless, unfulfilled, and discontent with the life-circumstances the Lord has placed before us. We may begin to doubt Him and His character.

On the other hand, there are those of us who are too fearful of stepping out in pursuit of something new—or anything, really. Out of a fear of failure, we may dismiss any outside opportunities to use our God-given gifts. We are told to lay down our lives for the sake of Christ, and we assume that means laying down everything we are good at, passionate about, or gifted with. Death-to-self supposedly means death-to-dreams, and we choose to die to anything that makes our souls stir, labeling all personal desires as selfish or sinful. Where the world says to go chase a passion no matter the cost, some of us assume that the godly alternative is to simply deny our passions altogether. When it comes to ambition or pursuit or dream-chasing or whatever you want to call it, some of us assume the world always says *yes* and the Christian always says *no.*

Beyond the exhaustion, frustration, and inner conflict that can easily result from wholeheartedly pursuing a dream, I believe there are eternal consequences at stake when we trust in the successes of our dream—or even the denial of it—to bring true happiness and fulfillment. Whether it's going after it with all we have or killing it in its tracks, in both cases, *what we do with a dream* can end up being our sole focus, the place where we look for satisfaction instead of God. Whether we pursue or deny, we may be so busy building our kingdoms here that we never live for the kingdom to come.

So how do we know if we should pursue a dream? Are we dreaming too big? Are we dreaming too small? Is dreaming at all a totally selfish endeavor, or is it okay in certain situations? How do we navigate whether or not we should move forward with an idea that we just can't seem to shake? Because our culture (and its values and norms) drastically changes over time, the answers to these questions will inevitably vary from generation to generation. Ask a millennial about pursuing dreams and then ask someone who was alive during the Great Depression. You will surely get two very different responses.

The questions we should be asking are: *What is the biblical approach to dreaming and how do we know if our dream is in God's will?* While there is not a one-size-fits-all answer to this (something the messaging all around us falsely tells us there is), while each one of us is called to a different life with different circumstances, and while God's Word may not address your dream specifically, there's one thing we can be sure of in this dream-chasing world: Scripture does provide trustworthy wisdom to help the Christian navigate when to move forward or not. This is the beauty of the Bible: its wisdom is timeless and is 100-percent relevant despite the changing norms, values, expectations, and trends of every type of culture. The answers to our questions are indeed found within its pages.

I charged hard toward my goals even as God closed doors and redirected my steps. I experienced frustration and inner turmoil along the way. I felt the deep longing to be identified by the dream I was chasing after. Contrary to the mantra that you can make anything happen if you work hard enough and simply get out of your own way, I found myself facing a lot of *nos* from God. Other times I faced a *pause* or a *wait.* And still other times, I was called to *pursue*—to go for it. In all of these yeses, nos, and waits, and in His perfect timing, God set me on a new path—one that led to something far beyond anything I could have imagined for myself. He used the ups and downs of my journey to reveal to me that true fulfillment and life purpose is found in Him alone. And though He certainly didn't have to, in the end, He tied in all the things I was passionate about early into my entrepreneurial journey and wove them into a ministry that allows others to pursue their passions and dreams too. Your story will look different than mine, but my prayer for you is that this book points you to Jesus and helps you discern the next step.

A Holy Pursuit aims to remind you of who you are in Christ first and then to encourage you to use the truth and hope of the gospel as a lens when pursuing a dream. God knows the desires of our hearts because God is the One who created us. He knows us intimately and is well aware of that dream or idea impressed on your heart right now, but His ultimate desire is for His people to love Him wholeheartedly, obey His commands, and seek after His will.

Dive into Scripture alongside me as we consider the biblical approach to dreaming. I believe that by truly understanding the implications of Christ's work on the cross for us, we have the freedom to move forward with, press pause on, or lay down the dreams stirring within us.

Chapter 1

THE WAY THE WORLD DOES DREAMING

"Satan has been a liar from the beginning. His constant goal is to get believers to turn their backs on the promises of God and pursue apparently rosier dreams."[1]

—Iain Duguid

It was a blessing and a curse to attend college in Clearwater, Florida. I was born and raised in the brutally cold (yet beautiful) land of Wisconsin and, therefore, a life of constant warmness was my college dream. However, it was difficult to sit in a chilly, sterile classroom as the warm rays of sunshine teased me about what was outside that window. It was all too easy to lose myself in thoughts about the future as I zoned out, looking through the glass. And then the scratching of pencils or feverish typing on laptops brought me back to the reality of smeared chalk on the back side of my professor (unbeknownst to him) as he spouted off scientific jargon I couldn't understand. My dreams would have to wait until I was done with school.

As a second-semester transfer, I felt awkward entering a new campus in the middle of the year at a small Christian college. There were only a handful of students, and everyone noticed the new kids. "What's your major?" remained the go-to get-to-know-you question I was often asked. I would almost always respond with, "English education, but one day I hope to own a photo studio." I carried my entry-level DSLR camera around often, so it wasn't completely unusual for me to throw in that disclaimer. However, despite my quick and confident answer, I questioned my response every time I said it. My internal monologue would ask, "How does an English ed. major get from teaching to owning a studio?"

The path that led me to pick an education major is an interesting one. I can't help but laugh when I reflect on my first-grade dreams. During one classroom ice-breaker game, our teacher asked us what we wanted to be when we grew up. Doctor. Movie star. President. These were the responses of my classmates. I, however, just wanted to be a cashier. Everyone laughed when they heard the simplicity of my answer. I loved playing pretend store. My friend from across the street would use her dad's old auto sales receipt pads from his work, and we would sell cars, homes, and eventually, lemonade. (Little did I know that the future days of self-checkout would allow me to live out this dream over and over again.) But that pursuit was too simple. And I would soon feel the pressure of figuring out what I wanted to do with my life.

I excelled in my studies until I transferred to a private school in ninth grade. In this school, our grades were less about projects and presentations, and more focused on quizzes and tests. I struggled with that form of assessment and it was not long before I traded an interest in good grades for an interest in popularity. I spent most of my high school career headed down a destructive path—trying to find happiness in friends, shopping, and boyfriends. Praise the Lord for His intervention! In conjunction with the love and patience of my parents, the persistent prayers and listening ears of Miss K—a young, passionate twenty-something English teacher—who the Lord used to draw me out of a life enslaved to sin and into the freedom found in Christ.

In the middle of our choir trip, we watched a movie on the bus followed by a discussion with Miss K in her hotel room. She encouraged us to examine our own hearts, and it was in those moments I knew I was not a Christian. Though outwardly I tried to display some form of moral living, inwardly I had been living my own life apart from God, and that lifestyle destroyed me. Once I got back to my room, I cried out to God in the middle of the bathroom floor. I confessed my sin and my need for a Savior, and asked God to be the Lord of my life. I committed the entirety of my life to Him. God used Miss K to reverse the trajectory of my life, and I wanted to do the same for others. So, like her, I decided to become an English education major. A new dream had formed.

The problem with attempting to copy and paste another person's life story is the simple fact that their story is not your story. I appreciated literature but I really struggled with grammar in college, and eventually realized that I may not be cut out to be an English education major. My heart really belonged with photography, but I made my career decision based on what would "have the most impact" and what I thought my parents would support. And this is what led me to walk around campus, torn between two careers, spouting the confusing English-education-plus-photo-studio-dream story.

Plans changed again when I met my husband, Ethan. He was on the opposite corner of the United States, stationed in Washington. His cousin was my roommate, and we connected through social media when he saw pictures of her and me together. Our first date began at the airport and ended a few days later after he visited me. Things moved quickly, and before I knew it, we were in love, engaged, married, and living in Washington state by age twenty. Moving meant transferring schools and I was not sure I wanted to continue with English education. My ambitions had gone from future cashier to popular girl to Christian-English-major to this new phase of life. I was at a crossroads once again seeking God's "purpose" for my life while trying to figure out how my giftings and desires would fit into His plan.

This way of thinking isn't far off from what many people struggle with. Graduating high schoolers go through the same process I did, wondering what major they should choose. Determined to make an impact, they lean heavily toward one major. Concerned about salary, they switch to another. But impact and salary alone aren't enough to fuel four-plus years of your head buried in books while living on a ramen-noodle budget. And so, some start from scratch and opt for the thing they were always passionate about. Others don't, and live life wondering, "What if?"

This confusion isn't just for high school and college students. A single woman thriving in her career may wonder if Mr. Right will ever come along. And if and when he does, will his job and his dreams squelch hers? Will she be forced to move where he works? Will he even want her to work at all? And what if marriage isn't in the cards at all? What if?

Working moms wrestle with their call to pursue career for a variety of reasons including (but not limited to) solely supporting their families or helping supplement income. They may wrestle with internal guilt as they watch their stay-at-home mom friends share hourly updates about their one-on-one time with kids. They may worry over the effect day care or after-school programs may have on their children. Is it really okay to lean into community, letting the multifaceted "village" help raise their child? They may wonder also if they are allowed to truly love putting their hand to the particular plow God has gifted them for. Guilt looms overhead for liking their job. *What if I shouldn't like what I'm doing? What if I'm doing it all wrong? What if?*

On the other hand, the stay-at-home mom might wonder if she should start an in-home business or take part in local ministry on top of all she has been called to in the home. She wonders if investing in the needs right here in their home and neighborhood and church is enough. Shouldn't she be able to pull off more than this? Shouldn't she be out there making it happen like her working friends? She may worry about similar things with her own children: *Is being at home with one person all day enough for their social development? Are other kids in preschool getting more of "the village" experience than my kids are getting? Are we too isolated within these four walls—teaching my little ones that community isn't actually necessary? What if we are missing out somehow? What if?*

These are just examples, but I regularly engage with all sorts of women who are, in a word, restless. They went to school for one thing and ended up doing something entirely different. Some feel stuck and unfulfilled in lackluster careers while others are in the sometimes unglamorous trenches of motherhood. Both are seeking something "more." They feel the pressure too. "Dare to dream," they are told. "Invest in what makes you happy." The laundry pile before them doesn't make them happy. Their current bank account statement doesn't make them happy. Their task list at work doesn't make them happy. But maybe following their dream will make them happy. Perhaps the unrest they feel will be satisfied in the outcome of their goal. This is worldly thinking.

Not of the World

Worldly thinking is in direct opposition to biblical thinking. When I refer to thinking, what I mean is a person's worldview or ideology and the principles and doctrines that shape how they choose to live their lives. Whether a person believes in God or not, there is some sort of moral code we pattern our lives after.

A Christian's worldview and approach to life is built on the foundation of the Word of God, the Bible, and on the gospel of Jesus Christ, which Scripture calls the "wisdom of God," though it seems foolish to the world (1 Cor. 1:20–24). A non-Christian's worldview, however, is subjective and what the Bible calls foolish, though it seems wise to the world (Rom. 1:22). Their worldview may be built on another religion, another person's thoughts and philosophies, or it could be simply built on personal experience and emotion; in any case, they choose to do what is right in their own eyes (Prov. 21:2). The New Testament puts it this way:

> For though they knew God, they did not glorify him as God or show gratitude. Instead, their thinking became worthless, and their senseless hearts were darkened. . . . You should no longer live as the Gentiles live, in the futility of their thoughts. They are darkened in their understanding, excluded from the life of God, because of the ignorance that is in them and because of the hardness of their hearts. (Rom 1:21; Eph. 4:17–18)

But how did their thinking become so darkened, so worthless? There is a current, a stream of thinking that flows through the world that is headed by God's enemy, and is therefore against God's values and ways (Eph. 2:2). When those of the world reject God and His Word, they are falling prey to the enemy's tactics, and they deny the truth. As 2 Corinthians 4:4 says, Satan has "blinded the minds of the unbelievers to keep them from seeing the light of the gospel of the glory of Christ, who is the image of God." Because they are blinded to the truth, their advice, wisdom, and philosophies are in direct contrast with the Christian's lifestyle; therefore, our way of living—dreaming included—will look entirely different than the nonbeliever's way of living and dreaming.

Jesus made it clear that though we are sent *into* the world—where the course of thinking is against God—we are not to be *of* the world (John 17:14–19). Being "in" the world means we aren't supposed to run away from the world and those who are in it (John 17:15; 1 Cor. 5:9–10). After all, this world is our mission field. God made the earth good, and we can still live in it, enjoy it, and share the good news as we go about our lives.

The problem, then, comes when Christians go beyond simply living in the world for God's glory and become of the world—allowing worldly thinking to shape their belief system. We are explicitly told not to be conformed to the patterns of this world (Rom. 12:2).

Throughout Scripture, God calls His people to be holy or set apart. In the Old Testament, this looked like adhering to the laws God laid before them. "Be holy because I am holy" has always been the primary pursuit of His people (Lev. 11:45). And yet, Israel consistently sinned against God as they rejected His perfect law and allowed the pagan practices in the surrounding cultures to influence them. From idol worship to marriages outside of God's chosen people to disbelief and distrust in what God told them to do, their decisions to relax God's standards and cling to the wisdom of the day compromised their faith and resulted in rebellion. Jesus fulfilled the law perfectly in the New Testament, and holy living changed from a system of sacrifices to confessing that Jesus is Lord, committing your life to Him, and walking in His ways. However, worldly thinking affected the early church greatly too. A good chunk of the New Testament is spent encouraging the first Christians to "hold on to the pattern of sound teaching" and to "stand firm and hold fast to the traditions you were taught" (2 Tim. 1:13; 2 Thess. 2:15). Why? Because there were opportunists—preachers who taught the gospel "out of selfish ambition" and personal gain (Phil. 1:17). Others were deceivers—false teachers who intentionally tried to lead Jesus-followers astray (Matt. 24:24; Gal. 1:7). On top of this, there were also capitulators—those who simply gave up on faith in Christ when things got hard or when the world offered a seemingly better way to approach life.

Given all we see in Scripture and in the world around us, it is no surprise there remains an ongoing tension between God's truth and the world's lies. There always has been. Since God has called us to be set apart from the world, it is pertinent that not only our actions obey God's Word, but that our minds do as well.

Slow and Steady Fools the Church

A few years ago we moved into an 1850's farmhouse in Central Pennsylvania. During our second winter in the home, we noticed that our three kids appeared a little more dirty than usual. "When was the last time you gave the kids a bath?" Ethan asked me. I looked over at their cute, little faces and saw what looked like dirt on their chins and cheeks. Clearly, they had wiped something on their faces, but they are always playing hide-and-go-seek in closets or sneaking toys from our old, dusty attic, so it did not surprise me.

Sometime later, I spotted black grime clinging to the fringed ends of my woven wall hanging. I looked up to examine its surroundings, and then the cobwebs became much more apparent. I actually wondered if a new breed of spiders had taken over our house as all the webs were black and thick-looking.

"Ethan, do you remember us ever having spiders that spin black webs?" He couldn't recall.

One Sunday, we came home after church and heard the sirens from our carbon monoxide detectors. As I whipped open the front door, smoky fog with a distinct aroma seeped out. I told my kids to get back into the car until we could figure out what was going on. Praise the Lord, the house was not on fire. We opened the windows to air out the rooms, and when the smoke dissipated, Ethan ran downstairs to examine our furnace. He pulled off the pipe that connected the furnace to our chimney. Several feet of black soot, dirt, and debris fell out. These fumes did not just make our house dirty—they made our home deadly.

We never serviced our chimney in the two years we lived there. All sorts of unknowns (including chimney sparrows) had clogged our vent and rather than releasing the exhaust fumes, the clogged chimney forced them into our house. The filth in our home didn't just show up overnight. It was something that gradually seeped into the walls of our home, slow and steady, making its mark on walls and webs and wee ones. The warning signs were there, but we didn't take them seriously. And this is how lies, false teaching, destructive heresies—whatever you want to call it—work. Like the debris in our chimney, these lies slowly settle and compact until the air around is unbreathable, resulting in a deadly poison that has overtaken the church. And our present-day churches are littered with these worldly philosophies that Satan has slowly fed us for years.

We are naive if we think that the church today isn't susceptible to the deception of worldly thinking. Satan loves to deceive God's people, and he is good at it. Genesis 3 describes Satan as "the most cunning of all the wild animals that the LORD God had made" (v. 1). In Paul's letter to Ephesus, he admonishes them to "put on the full armor of God so that we can stand against the schemes of the devil" (Eph. 6:11). Why? Because we aren't fighting flesh and blood but rather the "cosmic powers over this present darkness, against the spiritual forces of evil in the heavenly places" (Eph. 6:12 ESV). This prowling lion is always on the move, plotting and seeking whom he can devour (1 Pet. 5:8). It is true that "there is nothing new under the sun" (Eccles. 1:9) and his attempts at corrupting God's holy purposes are old as time—literally.

Scripture tells us that it wasn't long after God created Adam and Eve that the serpent was in the garden using his smooth talk to attack God's order. Even before he says a word, we see that his plan of sabotage was already underway. He bypassed Adam and went straight to Eve, questioning God's Word and attempting to weaken her confidence in it when he says, "Did God actually say . . . ?" (Gen. 3:1 ESV).

Satan then goes onto say, "No! You will not die. . . . In fact, God knows that when you eat it your eyes will be opened and you will be like God, knowing good and evil" (vv. 4–5). This brief dialogue contains three distinct attacks against God and His word. The serpent insinuated that:

1. **God is a liar . . .** When the serpent said, "You will not die," he claimed that God didn't really mean what He said. *God isn't actually going to follow through with what He says and kill you.*

Not only did Satan undermine the character of God, but he also undermined the credibility of God's Word.

2. **. . . because God is trying to withhold something good from you.** *The real reason you can't eat it is because God is trying to keep something good from you. It must be of tremendous value if He is threatening to kill you if you eat it.* Again, Satan maligned the character of God in such a way that God appeared threatened by the knowledge a human being could have. Satan made it seem that God wasn't looking out for Adam and Eve's best interests after all.
3. **Therefore, God doesn't deserve to be obeyed.** *Because God is only looking out for number one, we can't really take Him seriously. Focus on yourself and discover the knowledge that awaits with one bite.* Satan implied that Adam and Eve's need to obey God was only as good as the reason He gave them to do so.

This is just one instance of Satan's manipulation, and this account sits right at the beginning of Scripture.

Simply having the head knowledge that Satan is actively working against God's good plan doesn't guarantee that his presence in the world is always obvious. From our perspective, we know the serpent is Satan and that Satan is terrible news. To Adam and Eve, he was just another animal under their care. He was sneaky. Have you ever seen a cartoon or movie where the main character comically consults an angel version of himself on one shoulder and a devil version of himself on the other? Satan doesn't unveil himself as a little red shoulder-buddy holding a pitchfork, trying to convince you that the evil path is better. Instead, he "disguises himself as an angel of light"

(2 Cor. 11:14), chooses to make the lie appear as truth, and uses others to do his work. Paul warns the early church in Acts 20:28–30:

> Be on guard for yourselves and for all the flock of which the Holy Spirit has appointed you as overseers, to shepherd the church of God, which he purchased with his own blood. I know that after my departure savage wolves will come in among you, not sparing the flock. Men will rise up even from your own number and distort the truth to lure the disciples into following them.

These wolves have a goal of intentionally drawing away followers of Christ. Jesus tells us that these false teachers will perform great signs and wonders which could very well deceive even the elect (Matt. 24:24). What a sad and scary thought that these people "will rise up even from your own number"! This isn't a random outside attack, but rather calculated destruction from within.

How can we be on guard for such people? The Epistles contain warning after warning to keep watch for false teachers and destructive heresies invading the church. Slow and steady lies fooled the first people on the planet and continue to fool the people of God today. Philippians 3:19 (ESV) alerts us: "Their end is destruction, their god is their belly, and they glory in their shame, with minds set on earthly things." Scripture says that these people are puffed up, full of conceit, and though they sound convincing, they know nothing of the true gospel and the life that pertains to godliness (1 Tim. 6:3–4, 7). These false teachers cannot bear fruit, and as we study the Word and grow in our relationship with God, asking Him for wisdom and discernment along the way, we will notice the subtle attacks founded on big lies.

Thomas Watson once said, "Satan's masterpiece, his dragnet by which he drags millions to hell, is to keep them in unbelief! He knows, if he can but keep them from believing the truth, he is sure to keep them from obeying it."[2] He aims to set our hearts on anything but God because his diabolical dream is to elevate his throne above God's. And one way he does that is by tainting the biblical perspective about how Christians should handle dreaming.

Lies the World Believes

Scroll briefly on Instagram or Pinterest, and you're sure to find some worldly wisdom. It is clear that the devil is actively seeking to thwart God's purposes, and therefore we should recognize his efforts to reject them. Perhaps some of these phrases are familiar to you:

1. Follow your heart.

You have most likely heard versions of this in a song or have seen it beautifully lettered on a sign. The call to follow our hearts takes us on an emotional path with no visible end in sight. The heart is fickle, and its desires lead us on a wild-goose chase. A form of this mantra might be, "If you're not passionate about it, don't do it." So, if you don't like your job, quit. If you want that promotion, get it at all costs. Go wherever your heart leads you. But this isn't limited to entrepreneurial pursuits and can fit into pretty much any other category of life. If you don't love your husband, divorce him. If you're not ready to be a parent, choose abortion. If what you're doing doesn't make you happy, stop and figure out what does.

But we know that "the heart is more deceitful than anything else, and incurable—who can understand it?" (Jer. 17:9). When I look back at many of my high school dating relationships, though I could not see it at the time, I recognize now that I should not have followed my heart. Trusting how I felt in the moment I paved several pathways to a broken heart. My own heart betrayed me over and over again. Has that ever happened to you in some way? Maybe it wasn't a dating relationship; maybe it was something else. But perhaps you too have gone after something with your whole heart, and you were so sincere in your efforts and belief in it, only to find out that you were sincerely wrong.

Rather than chasing after our fickle, wandering hearts, we should say along with hymn writer Robert Robinson, "Bind my wandering heart to thee."[3] Because we are prone to wander, we need to be anchored to the perfect, unchanging, and Holy God of this universe. The opposite of following our heart is: "Trust in the LORD with all your heart, and do not rely on your own understanding; in all your ways know him, and he will make your paths straight. Don't be wise in your own eyes; fear the LORD and turn away from evil" (Prov. 3:5–7). Where the world follows after their hearts, the Christian follows after the Lord. He is a better—a perfect—guide.

2. Chase after your dreams.

Freedom and happiness await those who follow their dreams, right? This lie guarantees fulfillment and joy if you chase after what you're passionate about. Perhaps for a season, the Christian might find some short-term fulfillment in the pursuit of a dream, but ultimately, he or she will become enslaved to the very thing they are pursuing and will have given their whole heart to it. Has this ever happened to you? If so, I'm sure the book of Ecclesiastes was a great reference to you as it was to me when considering the fleeting pursuits of this world. The author is painfully aware of the Fall and attempts to satisfy himself through worldly pleasures. But each attempt at worldliness and self-gratification turns out to be "vanity and a striving after wind" (Eccles. 4:4 ESV). You can have that dream job, all those Instagram followers, and a wardrobe to match, but if God is not your true source of joy and fulfillment, anything apart from Him will not satisfy.

Why? Because man was not made to be satisfied by the created things of this world but rather by the Creator of all things. The final verdict of Ecclesiastes says, "Fear God and keep his commandments, for this is the whole duty of man. For God will bring every deed into judgment, with every secret thing, whether good or evil" (Eccles. 12:13b–14). Here is the bottom line: freedom and happiness await those who fear God and keep His commandments.

3. Go make a difference in this world.

Wait, what is wrong with making a difference in the world? This one may not be as obvious, but the underlying premise is somewhat unclear. Who defines what makes a difference? By what standard is the difference made? The problem is that making a difference becomes something measurable, something immediately seen.

The opposite side of this lie would be this: if you can't visibly see results, then you're probably not making a mark in this world. For example, if I start a nonprofit company that provides job training and a steady income to women in a third world country, I am making a difference. That difference is seen every time that woman brings home money to support and raise her family. This is a noble pursuit, and I've been encouraged by the many men and women in this world whose visible impact has changed lives. However, the problem occurs when we place value on the change we can see happening now and with that, we devalue anything that doesn't display immediate change or fruit—which is most things. The vast majority of the time, fruit takes time to grow.

Motherhood, for example, isn't a calling where we necessarily see an immediate, measurable difference. When I tell my children it's time for them to go to bed and they groan and complain all the way up to their bedroom the same way they did last night (and the night before), I do not see measurable difference. I may not feel like I'm changing the world if I were to consider my daily routine, but the faithfulness of a mother in those mundane moments cultivates a sense of security and love deep within a child's heart that may not reap a reward for years to come.

Colossians 3:23–24 encourages us: "Whatever you do, do it from the heart, as something done for the Lord and not for people, knowing that you will receive the reward of an inheritance from the Lord. You serve the Lord Christ." Rather than working to make an impact, we work as unto the Lord. Both the nonprofit owner and the mother can joyfully serve the Lord and leave the results to Him. Yes, we strive to change the world. But we let God define the pace in how He uses us to do that, which might be slower than our culture has patience for.

Lies the Christian Believes

Let's take this concept of worldly thinking a step further and consider two Christian versions with similar undertones but veiled in Christian jargon. At first read, you may see nothing wrong with these statements. Remember that our devil with a pitchfork looks more like an angel of light? Similarly, these statements don't shout at us—they whisper. They cajole. They're the subtle undertones that sneak into Christian thinking.

1. We can walk in freedom when we figure out God's purpose for our lives.

I met a woman who had prophecy spoken over her at a young age. We will call her Sarah. She was told she would do great things for the Lord through a particular vocation that God would lead her to. Now Sarah is a wife and mom and the words spoken over her have not been fulfilled. With tear-filled eyes, Sarah shared her discontent: "It feels like I'm not living out my purpose." My heart ached for her as I saw her obvious distress. I understand where she was coming from. It's easy to get lost in motherhood and question "purpose" but it pained me to hear her question her purpose when God was so clearly using her. She is an adoptive parent and loves children deeply. In the short time I've known her, I have listened to her pray fiercely over broken relationships in her family, and I witnessed her compassion as she gathered goods for a family in need. Alongside a few others, I was grateful to be able to encourage her in the areas I see God using her throughout her home and community. I reminded her that her life is not defined by some words spoken over her as a child but rather in the new identity given as a child of God. It made me wonder, though, how many Christians are still searching for their purpose or feel that they have missed out on it altogether?

I have seen versions of this "find your God-given purpose and find freedom" mind-set shared on Instagram and tucked into blog posts. It is suggested that if you are feeling burnt out, unfulfilled, or overwhelmed, then you must not be living out God's purpose. Statements like this lead us to think that we potentially could be living out a purpose that God didn't intend for us. This is why a wounded spouse might think, "Did I marry the person God intended for me?" or a Christian working a job that feels neither meaningful nor fulfilling might ask, "Am I at the right job?" We all have stressful days or dry seasons of life, but are these accurate indicators of purposelessness? No. Our purpose is clear: fear God and keep His commandments. We are to love the Lord our God with all our heart, soul, mind, and strength, and we are to love our neighbors as ourselves (Eccles. 12:13b; Mark 12:30–31).

Do hardships reflect a life missing out on the freedom God intended for us? On the contrary, Scripture is filled with stories of hardship for the glory of God. Consider the lives of Joseph, Job, Daniel, Stephen, Paul—or even Jesus Himself! Each was called to different forms of suffering that I don't think any of us would wish upon anyone, and yet, each life feared God and kept His commandments in the ways God willed them to. What if any of these people simply gave up when things felt unflashy or unfulfilling? While yes, God does lead us forward in certain seasons of life to new jobs, or new towns, or new ministries, experiencing hardship is not the equivalent of God "calling" us away from right where we are. We must be wary of confusing discontentment and calling, and pray for the discernment to follow God wherever He's actually leading—whether that be moving on in a new season or staying put in an old one.

Additionally, does following our dreams bring lasting freedom? The only freedom we need is the freedom found in Christ. We once were enemies of God and children of wrath, but now we are no longer under a yoke of slavery to sin (Rom. 5:10; 6:6). It is for freedom that Christ has set us free (Gal. 5:1)! *If you are a Christian, you are already walking in real, lasting freedom because Jesus broke our bondage to sin.* In Him, we have all joy, all purpose, and all fulfillment. Both the successful entrepreneur and the stay-at-home mom share the same freedom from sin if they are in Christ.

I want to say this loud and clear: it's nonsense to think that God's various callings on our lives give us any sort of liberation, as if by unlocking our own personal purpose there is some hidden mystery yet to be revealed to us. Scripture does not support this, and we need to guard our minds against such destructive thinking. That successful entrepreneur may lose his or her business, and that mother may lose her child, but their identities are fixed in their Savior. They can be "afflicted in every way but not crushed; we are perplexed but not in despair; we are persecuted but not abandoned; we are struck down but not destroyed" (2 Cor. 4:8–9). They can still rejoice because their identity rests not in their calling or their dream, but in the *God* of our past, present, and future.

When we say things like, "This is my purpose in life," as if something other than glorifying God and proclaiming the gospel to all nations holds greater weight in our lives, then we are trusting in our dreams for freedom and not trusting in God. He is the peace that passes all understanding; He is the source of all goodness. He is all the freedom we need. Both freedom and purpose are a result of the gospel—not a result of following our dreams.

2. Our ability to impact the kingdom of God depends on finding God's purpose.

There is that *impact* word again. I read a statement very much like this on a major Christian organization's conference page: their heart is to help you discover your true purpose so that you can live your fullest potential on this earth. This sounds like a positive statement, but once we unpack the deeper meanings, we see that this is another harmful pattern of thinking for the believer. This is similar to the previous statement in that it also calls into question God's individual purposes in our lives. It claims that when we find our God-given purpose, then we can "go make a difference" in this world. It's pertinent that we understand that God's kingdom is not dependent on His people figuring out their purpose. The advancement of God's kingdom is dependent on *God*—on the work of the Holy Spirit moving and transforming hearts. We are merely the vessels God uses. It has never been our God-given gifts, abilities, or words that have had the power to give new birth to souls. This is why Paul never preached with fancy verbiage; he didn't want his hearers' faith to rest in man's wisdom or ability, but rather the power of God (1 Cor. 2:4). Our ability to impact anything always rests in the power of God and not ourselves.

Again, who determines what "impact for the kingdom of God" looks like anyway? Imagine Joseph—who had faithfully served in Potiphar's home and was falsely accused of attacking Potiphar's wife—sitting in a prison cell considering the impact he was making in the world. Did being sold into slavery by his own family make a difference in the world? Were the false accusations by Potiphar's wife that landed him in prison making a difference in the world? Joseph didn't run around chasing after his heart or attend a conference to unlock his purpose; he simply trusted in the Lord and remained obedient in every circumstance God helped him to endure. His faith in God is further expressed when Joseph acknowledged that the evil done to him was used for good by God to save lives (Gen. 50:20). The visible result was a significant number of lives being saved, yes, but it took many years before that reason was ever revealed. And don't forget: Joseph had no way of knowing that was going to be the outcome! Yet he still honored God right where he was. Like the lives of many other faithful servants of God, Joseph's journey reflected a "walk by faith" attitude as opposed to a "find out what you're here for and go make an impact" kind of attitude.

When It All Comes Back to Me

What do all of these modern-day mantras have in common? They are all centered on *me* and *my* own self-fulfillment. The happiness or freedom I desire points to me, flows from me, and often the primary person to benefit is me. We end up bearing the burden for our own joy and worth, and the result is likely frustration when the formula doesn't equate the way these mantras promise. A life focused on self is not at all the life God calls Christians to (Matt. 16:24–25). This is usually a good filter for determining if something you're reading or listening to falls more in line with secular thinking than biblical thinking: Who does it point to? Who does this flow from? Who does it benefit? Is this consistent with what is revealed in Scripture? If any of these do not check out, then we ought to be concerned with the inspiration and advice we allow to permeate in our hearts and shape our thinking and living.

It is Satan's aim to corrupt God's holy purposes for this world—chasing dreams included—and we must be on guard. The best way to navigate through his attempts at sabotaging even the good things in our lives is to ensure that we have proper biblical framework guiding our lives. Like glasses that help those who need to see clearly, it is crucial that the dreamer (and all Christians, for that matter) gain proper perspective.

I recently went to the doctor in search of the root cause for some ongoing medical issues. After getting a full panel of bloodwork in multiple categories, the results came back, and my doctor said, "You are healthy! Everything looks wonderful, and I see nothing to worry about." I couldn't understand why I was so lethargic. I wasn't pregnant. My thyroid and iron levels were ideal. It wasn't long after, my husband and I cut sugar and carbs out of our diet entirely. Two weeks into this lifestyle change and I had more energy than what even a good cup of coffee could deliver. It made sense. I had been fueling myself with junk for so long. Sugar, in particular, wasn't just found in the bag of Milano cookies I snuck tastes of between every meal; it's also found in our bread, salad dressings, and even shows up in many raw meats. Cutting it out and fueling myself with clean food was a game-changer; the results were felt immediately. In the same way, for us to maintain a proper biblical outlook, we must evaluate what fuels us. We have to look at what's going in our hearts before we can rightly use what's coming out of our lives for God's glory.

Preached in 1982 and still relevant today, John Piper words it well:

> Satan devotes himself 168 hours a week trying to deceive you and fill your mind with junk. He has seen to it that you are surrounded almost entirely by Christless culture whose mood, and entertainment, and advertising, and recreation, and politics are shot through with lies about what you feel and think and do. Do you think that in this atmosphere you can maintain a vigorous, powerful, free, renewed mind with a ten-minute glance at God's book once a day?[4]

Do we recognize that Satan is on the hunt and wants to take our focus off God and put it on ourselves? What music, books, or TV shows am I filling myself with? What messages am I allowing to permeate my brain? Are my go-to sources of inspiration pithy quotes that sound true but really proclaim worldly lies? Daily we consume some sort of philosophy or agenda. The commercials we watch, the podcasts we listen to, the people we follow on Twitter and Instagram are all shaped by their belief system, and when we choose to give them a foothold in our lives by listening or reading, we open ourselves to persuasion that is potentially detrimental to our spiritual health. Again, I'm not saying we need to avoid the world. We are called to live in it and minister to it. But when worldly thinking becomes so second nature to us that we can't even detect its presence in our minds, something's very wrong.

Throughout the diet Ethan and I were on, we discovered that the health aisle is not very trustworthy. Though there are countless products labeled "organic," "low-carb," or "sugar-free," when we looked at the nutrition labels, we discovered these items were deceptive. The valid identifier of whether or not the products are actually beneficial for your body is in the nutrition label. To read a nutrition label, you have to know what to look for. How many net carbs are in it? How much sugar? What ingredients did they sneak in? A chocolate bar may label itself as sugar-free and yet contain sucralose or maltodextrin, which are forms of sugar.

Similarly, perhaps many of the books, podcasts, or online sermons that are part of our regular diet are labeled "Christian" or appear "Christian" but, as we can, see that word is not always a guarantee. While there is no nutrition label to refer to, we can weigh their words against Scripture. Like the Bereans, we can examine Scripture to see if their words line up with biblical truth (Acts 17:11). To catch the subtle contradictions, we must have an intimate knowledge of our Bibles. Piper argues that ten minutes a day in our Bibles is not enough, and I have to agree.

Desiring God's Word

The psalmist throughout Psalm 119 exemplifies what it looks like to live guided and directed by the truth of God's Word. The entire psalm is worth reading and meditating on, but we will focus in on the instruction found in verses 1–8:

> How happy are those whose way is blameless,
> who walk according to the LORD's instruction!
> Happy are those who keep his decrees
> and seek him with all their heart.
> They do nothing wrong;
> they walk in his ways.

You have commanded that your precepts
be diligently kept.
If only my ways were committed
to keeping your statutes!
Then I would not be ashamed
when I think about all your commands.
I will praise you with an upright heart
when I learn your righteous judgments.
I will keep your statutes;
never abandon me.

1. Following God's Instruction Results in True Happiness

One thing I've noticed consistently in pet ownership is that animals love to push their boundary lines. No matter where we've lived, no matter how big or small the yard size, our dogs have always attempted to go beyond the fences that protect them from what awaits them on the other side. When we moved to our farmhouse, we thought that surely the couple acres that came with it would give them enough space and freedom to do whatever dogs like to do. But even still, they run right up to the fence line and seek out methods of escape.

Do they think the grass is greener on the other side? Do they believe we are withholding better lands to sniff or grass to roll in? It may seem like our boundary lines are restrictive and holding them back from true freedom, but the reality is that we fenced off our yard to protect them (and our kids) from the many tractors and farm equipment that pass back and forth our house daily.

Sadly, on the first night of moving into our home, our two dogs decided to make their way out to that road, and with tear-filled eyes and heavy hearts, we buried one of them shortly after. What our dogs don't see or understand is that within the perimeters of our home, there is safety from certain dangers of this world. Not only do they have protection, but we have food and water for them daily, loving family members to play with them, and a warm home for them to sleep in. Our rules are not intended to withhold joy but rather to provide it under the shelter of our love and care.

But dogs don't see it that way, do they? They don't see that the grass is greener right here, with their food and their water and their acres to run and their people. No. All they see is the fence—the killjoy, the boundary line that doesn't let them wander into what they assume is greener pastures.

The world has a similar mentality toward God's instruction. It sees any one of His boundary lines as a killjoy—a bunch of rules that take all the fun out of life. It believes the age-old lie from Satan, that God is restricting us from attaining true happiness. But the first two verses of Psalm 119 boldly challenge this line of thinking. They tell us that the person who keeps God's instructions, keeps His decrees, and seeks after Him with their whole heart is happy. Right away a promise is given to us: be blameless and follow the Lord's instruction and you will be happy. Let's refer back to verse 4, "You have commanded that your precepts be diligently kept." If happiness is following God's instruction and God's instruction (or command) is that His precepts be diligently kept, then it is possible for us to have the attitude of verses 6–8 which say, "Then I would not be ashamed when I think about all your commands. I will praise you with an upright heart when I learn your righteous judgments. I will keep your statutes; never abandon me." In other words, this isn't some half-hearted obedience—no, the psalmist is all in. He recognizes that the by-product of obedience to God is happiness. These claims stand in contrast with the idea that chasing after our dreams, reaching our goals, and making things happen will fulfill us. Instead, these verses show us that chasing *God* in His *Word* is what fulfills us.

2. Following God's Command Guards Us against Sin

Let's continue in Psalm 119:9–11:

> How can a young man keep his way pure?
> By keeping your word.
> I have sought you with all my heart;
> don't let me wander from your commands.
> I have treasured your word in my heart
> so that I may not sin against you.

It's interesting how often I see a T-shirt or hand-lettered print that says, "Prone to wander . . ." as if it is a good thing. Someone somewhere decided to play on these old words from Mr. Robinson's hymn and apply them to the wanderlust mentality our generation is so consumed with. It's popular phrases like these that reveal how little our culture regards original context. The original hymn says, "Prone to wander, Lord, I feel it. Prone to leave the God I love."[5] Knowing the original intent, this isn't my first choice of words to wear on a T-shirt or hang in my home—even if the new meaning is wanderlust. For as much as I know the truth and still feel tempted to move God down on the priority list, I am not alone in my tendency to wander away from God. How can I fight that which I'm naturally prone to?

Keeping God's Word protects us from falling into sin. Verse 9 asks the question and then answers it: How can we maintain purity? By keeping His Word. Psalm 37:31–33 says, "The instruction of his God is in his heart; his steps do not falter. The wicked one lies in wait for the righteous and intends to kill him; the Lord will not leave him in the power of the wicked one or allow him to be condemned when he is judged." Scripture affirms yet again that the evil one seeks to destroy the righteous, and yet, one major weapon against his attacks is the Word of God. Because God's instruction is in his heart "his steps do not falter." This psalmist understands that the one who keeps God's Word or clings to God's instruction protects himself from wandering off into sin. Therefore, we should pray as the psalmist does, "Don't let me wander from your commands" (119:10). And when we pray this, we are not only fighting against sin, we are admitting the reality that God *Himself* has a part to play in our obedience to His Word, as we will see in the principle below.

3. Following God's Commands Requires the Help of God

There was a season in my Christian walk where I grew inconsistent with my Scripture reading. I became so upset with myself because I had the head knowledge of what I should do but had no inward desire to do it. I decided to turn to Psalm 119 as a reminder of Scripture's value, but rather than just reading why it is profitable, it revealed that even my very desire for it comes from Him.

"Turn my eyes from looking at what is worthless; give me life in your ways" (v. 37). That verse was a mirror of my own heart. I was consumed with worthless things, but I need not stay there. The psalmist asked God to give him life—to pull him out of the muck and mire and set him upon the path of life. And so, I prayed through this psalm with fresh eyes.

There is a clear plea from the psalmist to God, acknowledging in utter humility how much he needs God in the process of keeping His commands, attaining blessing or happiness, and keeping away from sin.

Verses 17–19 acknowledge his neediness:

> Deal generously with your servant
> so that I might live;
> then I will keep your word.
> Open my eyes so that I may contemplate
> wondrous things from your instruction.
> I am a resident alien on earth;
> do not hide your commands from me.

The psalmist made three requests: "deal generously with your servant," "open my eyes," and "do not hide your commands." And if we look at the verses we have already covered we read: "never abandon me" (v. 8) and "don't let me wander" (v. 10). The psalmist's abilities to live out God's commands come from God. Each statement he makes is preceded with a request from God to help him. "*Deal generously with your servant . . . then I will keep your word. Open my eyes that I may contemplate* wondrous things from your instruction." If we continued reading this psalm, we find dozens of requests:

- "*Help me* understand the meaning . . ." (v. 27)
- "*Strengthen me* through your word . . ." (v. 28)
- "*Keep me* from the way of deceit . . ." (v. 29)
- "Graciously *give me* your instruction . . ." (v. 29)
- "*Do not put me* to shame . . ." (v. 31)
- "*You broaden* my understanding . . ." (v. 32)
- "*Teach me,* LORD, the meaning . . ." (v. 33)
- "*Help me* understand . . ." (v. 34)
- "*Help me* stay on the path . . ." (v. 35)
- "*Turn my heart* to your decrees . . ." (v. 36)

On and on and on we could go all the way through the entire 176 verses. This psalmist clearly needs God's power to help him love and obey God! And so do we. We cannot muster it on our own. What encouragement that our ability to serve God does not rest in our own strength. This is the theme of all Scripture, and the very heart of the gospel! He created us, He chose us, He saved us, He sustains us, He sanctifies us, and it's all for His glory. It's all from Him, for Him, to Him, and if we want to live a life for His glory, we must humble ourselves and recognize just how much we need Him to help us.

As we grow consistent in our Bible reading, develop a true love in chasing God through it, and ask Him to help us along the way, He will give us eyes to see the various ways that the enemy is out to destroy us and distort the way we perceive God and His truth. This will help us separate ourselves from the world—not just in our actions but in our thinking. The world is quick to tell us how we should live and how we should dream, and if we are not careful, we may start believing the lie that happiness is found within our dreams—whether apart from God or even with Him. We must cautiously examine the information we absorb and test it against the Scriptures because we know that God demands Christians live differently than the people who reject Him.

The only way to successfully do this is to allow the power of the Holy Spirit to equip us with discernment as we seek the truth found in God's Word. *Does what I'm reading or hearing line up with what Scripture says?* God's Word must be the final authority in our lives—and the authority over our dreams—and we must turn to it regularly. Not Instagram. Not podcasts. Not catchy sermon phrases. Not hand-lettered quotes. Not the inside advice of influencers. May we not be deceived; may we walk in obedience because of who God is and what His Word says. There's no better way to close this chapter than with the words of Paul himself:

> Finally, be strengthened by the Lord and by his vast strength. Put on the full armor of God so that you can stand against the schemes of the devil. For our struggle is not against flesh and blood, but against the rulers, against the authorities, against the cosmic powers of this darkness, against evil, spiritual forces in the heavens. For this reason, take up the full armor of God, so that you may be able to resist in the evil day, and having prepared everything, to take your stand. Stand, therefore, with truth like a belt around your waist, righteousness like armor on your chest, and your feet sandaled with readiness for the gospel of peace. In every situation take up the shield of faith with which you can extinguish all the flaming

arrows of the evil one. Take the helmet of salvation and the sword of the Spirit—which is the word of God. Pray at all times in the Spirit with every prayer and request and stay alert with all perseverance and intercession for all the saints. (Eph. 6:10–18)

Chapter 2

WHEN GOD BECOMES YOUR GENIE AND YOUR DREAMS BECOME YOUR GOD

"We resemble what we revere, either for ruin or restoration."[1]

—G. K. Beale

My mom has very few pictures of her childhood in the Philippines. She grew up in a culture completely opposite to mine, but her incredible stories paired with the few film photographs of her family fueled my imagination as I envisioned her as a young girl. From the disposable cameras I carried in grade school to the brick-sized digital camera I frequently borrowed from my parents in high school, I documented everything I did not want to forget so my future kids would have visuals to match my stories, just as I had with my mom's pictures.

Toward the end of my senior year of high school, I came across some online images that a former schoolmate of mine had posted. Her images looked far different than the photos I had taken on our point-and-shoot camera. The pictures had depth. The colors were vibrant, and the subjects stood apart from their backgrounds. Her photographs not only introduced me to the world of DSLR cameras, but also helped me view photography as an art form. My love for this medium grew even more.

The big dilemma remained whether I would continue with my major or pursue what I was really head over heels for. Ethan could see the turmoil brewing within me. He knew it was my mom's desire for me to finish college with a bachelor's degree, but he also knew how happy I was behind the camera. Continuing with the education major didn't sit right with me, and after discovering a degree in photography at a community college, we found a compromise that would please my parents and allow me to pursue my real passion. He understood that it would take time to establish a business and did not mind being a single-income family so I could chase my dream of working as a photographer. Even though I would not work in an environment where I could build relationships the way a teacher could, I sought out ways that I could use photography to glorify God.

God gave me many opportunities to serve Him and gain experience while stationed in Washington. Our church asked me to teach a photography-basics class to refugees who were forced to relocate to the area. Over a dozen women attended the course. They could not understand me, and I could not understand them, but we communicated via smiles and hand gestures. Despite the language barrier, it was a blessing to work with these women. I also photographed a few military events and local military families, which helped me practice my skills and grow my portfolio. Additionally, I took a college film course that required me to shoot manually with a 35mm camera, develop my own rolls of film, and print my own work. All the while, I booked my first few weddings to gain experience in the niche I wanted to pursue: wedding photography.

But I was hungry to learn more. When I wasn't shooting or editing, I took in whatever knowledge I could about photography and the wedding industry. I kept up with blog posts from well-known photographers, and studied what was trending. I carefully examined the methods of my favorite photographers in an attempt to discover what led to their success. *What is it about their photos that I love? What about the experience they offered made their clients love them? How do they set themselves apart in an increasingly over-saturated market?*

If photography were like dating, I must have had a specific "type." As I studied the details of their lives, I was always surprised when I discovered that my favorite photographers turned out to be Christians who lived in California. I dreamed of someday meeting them, attending a workshop, and eventually being like them.

Around our six-month wedding anniversary, the military gave us orders to move from Washington state to California. The sunshine was calling my name once again, but I was even more excited that we were headed to the land where all the well-known artists I obsessed over lived and worked. I was sure that the Lord wanted me to become a wedding photographer and that this move would surely pave the way for that dream to come true.

Not even a few days after our move, I connected with a talented Christian photographer I met online. I was a stranger to this new place and everyone in it, and she became my first friend. Not only did she introduce me to the glorious wonders of Ikea, Thai food, and bubble tea, but she also taught me a lot about business, client experience, and the photography industry in general. I had many opportunities to assist her and practice my skills under her guidance. In those first months, we attended several workshops and events together. I ate, slept, and breathed the craft, and every weekend I searched for something photography-related to fill my time.

And then my favorite photographer of that time, Jasmine Star, came to our town for a speaking engagement. If photographers had their own world of celebrities, she was the "It Girl." To say I was starstruck was an understatement. Before her workshop started, she announced that she forgot her camera and needed someone to take pictures of the event. She spiced things up by turning this into a challenge. Whoever submitted the best photo would win a years worth of web hosting, in addition to a shout out and feature on her blog. The thought thrilled me. While everyone was busy grabbing shots of Jasmine teaching, I tried to think outside of the box. I focused my attention on her husband's expressions. He smiled with pride as she talked about her own photographic journey and motivated everyone in the room to pursue theirs. At one point she made a joke, and it was then I snapped a candid shot of his reaction. She loved the image and selected me to be one of the winners. This was yet another "sign" or confirmation that I was exactly where I was supposed to be. Right?

Just a week later, I attended another free photography event when a woman sitting behind me tapped me on the shoulder and said, "Are you Dianne Jago?" My inward reaction was a mixture of pride and skepticism. *Why, yes, I am—wait, who wants to know?* "You were the one who won Jasmine Star's contest?!" Indeed, I was. The photography world grew smaller. I soaked in that little taste of glory for the rest of the weekend. It felt good to be known. It felt good to be seen. It felt good to be identified with something I loved. This kind of glory was addicting.

From this point forward, the hopes and dreams I had for myself consumed me. I tried to do as much as I could in my own strength to make things happen. I attended networking parties, volunteered at local events, and reached out to as many established photographers as I could seek out opportunities to assist and be mentored. In the process, however, I wrestled with bouts of depression and frustration as I watched other local photographers publish all the beautiful shoots they were commissioned to do. From my perspective, their successes revealed my failure; another's booked client represented an opportunity I had missed. While there were a few breaks that came my way, they were not enough. The glory from those moments did not last long, and I did not have enough bookings to keep me too busy to notice. I longed for attention that never satisfied. That desire drove me to accumulate more clients, more followers, and a passion for more notoriety. I went through waves of emotion blaming myself, blaming others, and eventually asking God why all the pieces did not fit together as I expected they would.

Scribbled in the middle of my journal I wrote about a deep fear that my plans might not come to fruition: "I have no promise that I'll get to where I want to be and that scares me." I did not want to even consider photography to be outside of His will for my life. Therefore, every positive aspect of my business was counted as a sign that I should be doing this and anything else was disregarded. I held on tightly to my dream and refused to let it go.

When God Becomes Your Genie

I had the head knowledge that the Lord was in control of all things, including my dreams. I knew that He was the one directing events in my life, and my lack of clients and slow-growing business was because He willed it to be so. And so, I began praying more and more about the dream I had for myself. My prayers became less about spending time with God and more about venting my frustrations and handing Him my list of demands. Of course, I would throw in the disclaimer: "Your will be done." But I treated God more as a your-wish-is-my-command type of genie rather than addressing a holy God worthy of prayers formed from adoration, confession, petition, and thanksgiving. All my religious-speak and ultimatums and tantrums were really just ways I was trying to rub the lamp just right. If I could offer the right words and fake some sort of good perspective, maybe God would pop out, cave in, and grant me my dream. Like Aladdin's genie, maybe He'd make me a somebody.

Many of us are so swept off our feet by our dreams that our prayers shift from God-focused prayers to me-focused prayers. Charles Spurgeon, a wise preacher of the past, said that the weight of our prayers reflects our Christian walk. He explained that it is like a thermometer which indicates our spiritual temperature—it is not necessarily the length of our prayers but rather the intensity of our dependence on God in our prayer that serves as an evaluator of our spiritual walk.[2] If someone put a thermometer to my prayers, they would have found freezing temperatures, and a heart that cared more about growing my own kingdom than God's kingdom.

The more tightly I gripped my dream, the more the fear of losing it increased. This caused ongoing tension between my walk and wants. While there was a part of me that desired to be a fruitful Christian, I cared more about chasing my dreams and reaching my own goals. To be clear, there are many great dreams out there. Some long to be in a dating relationship, while others desire kids, for example, and those aren't bad dreams! They are God-given desires. But when our personal desires become a master, or a God-substitute, the desire is no longer good. At this point, it has become a god and needs to be dethroned. To preference our desires above His will for us is to reject His sole authority over our lives, whatever that outcome may be.

Jesus addresses this point quite clearly regarding material possessions versus trusting God for provision: "No one can serve two masters, since either he will hate one and love the other, or he will be devoted to one and despise the other . . ." (Matt. 6:24). The Pharisees He spoke of loved money so much that it kept them from serving their True Master. Have our dreams become our master? Are we slaves to our own pursuits?

When God is no longer preeminent in our lives, we develop a twisted and improper view of who He is. This ignorance of His supreme role in our lives leads us on a path that may have a Christian appearance on the surface, but inwardly leads us to our own emptiness and destruction. The result of dethroning God (which, bear in mind, is Satan's ultimate aim) places something or someone else on that throne. This is idolatry.

Of course, it's not very common for us to sit in a women's group and hear another sister in Christ vent, "Ladies, lately, I've really struggled with worshiping other gods." I remember learning the Ten Commandments as a young child. If asked, I would readily admit that I've lied before or wanted something that someone else had. But violating the command of Exodus 20:3, "Do not have other gods besides me"? Nope. I was fine there. The pagan gods mentioned throughout the Old Testament were foreign to me. The physical idols that Israel created as representations of God were clearly foolish. And because I didn't struggle with worshiping mythical gods or creating graven images, I did not concern myself with this commandment for many years to come. I actually thought to myself, *At least I don't have to worry about this one.*

I misunderstood that idolatry doesn't always take a primitive, tangible form like it did throughout the Old Testament. For example, Jesus said that a man who looks at a woman in lust has already committed adultery (Matt. 5:28). He may not have committed the physical act, but he is still guilty of an adulterous heart.

Similarly, we do not have to physically bow down in order to worship a false god. Idolatry occurs when we exalt something or someone else above God—the One who should have first place in our hearts and minds. Romans 1:21–25 gives a clear picture of man's natural tendency toward idolatry. This passage begins by saying "For though they knew God, they did not glorify him as God or show gratitude. Instead, their thinking became worthless, and their senseless hearts were darkened." Though mankind knows the truth, it still refuses to honor God the way He created it to. Therefore, they are turned over to worthless thinking. An incorrect view of God leads us on the path to idolatry as we no longer see Him for how we should worship Him. Paul continues in verse 22, "Claiming to be wise, they became fools and exchanged the glory of the immortal God for images resembling mortal man, birds, four-footed animals, and reptiles." What they think is wisdom is actually foolishness, and the result is God allowing those who reject Him to be turned over to their sin. "They exchanged the truth of God for a lie, and worshiped and served what has been created instead of the Creator, who is praised forever. Amen" (1:25). The idea of worshiping the created rather than the Creator is a theme that runs all throughout Scripture and it is exactly how the devil plots for us to turn our eyes away from true life and onto worthless things.

These truths revealed that a form of idolatry was, in fact, one of my greatest struggles and the source for so many other sins in my heart. In my clash of wills—God's will versus my will—I rejected His authority and developed a warped view of Him. He became more of a "genie" as the idol of photography took first place in my heart.

At some point, I had linked my successes to my relationship with God. I created an equation for the way our relationship worked, making it transactional instead of transformational. I thought if I did "X, Y, and Z" for God, then in return, He would bless me. Calculated human input guaranteed divine output. I figured if I maintained all the things a Christian should be doing like reading my Bible, getting involved in church, and prayer, then He would bless me with more clients. This was an exchange that I had set up in my mind that was not founded in Scripture, but instead, concocted by my own selfishness and idolatry. Even though there were points where I felt like I was in the right place with Him, my heart was far from Him and I did not know Him very well. For if I did, I would have known that He is not a vending machine where the right "input" will simply spit out a treat. He is not an equation one can manipulate or alter or figure out. He's a jealous God in covenant with me, the way a husband is desirous of the affections for his wife—and how I approached Him is not how He calls His people to love or serve Him.

I do not think there will be a day in this lifetime where I'm not battling to keep God as first priority in my life. And I'm probably not alone in that. After all, this sin has its origins in the garden when Adam and Eve chose something other than God to take first place in their hearts and actions. This ongoing struggle clearly continues throughout the Old and New Testaments. History repeats itself, and it's in our nature to follow the same mistakes as all who lived before us. "What has been is what will be, and what has been done is what will be done; there is nothing new under the sun" (Eccles. 1:9). Those in pursuit of a dream are prone to idolizing it. That doesn't mean that our pursuits, ambitions, or dreams are always necessarily bad. It means that we all, every single one of us, must be careful.

When Dreaming Meets Idolatry

Thinking about the possibilities of a dream reminds me of the early dating stages with my husband. When we first admitted our feelings to one another, I constantly thought about him, replaying the words we exchanged that day, evaluating how I felt in those moments, and imagining the next steps of our relationship. *Would he propose one day? Would we ever have kids? Where would we live and what will our lives look like?* There were butterflies. There was also fear of the unknown, but overriding any sort of worry was the hope for what was to come.

Dreams can have a similar effect on us. They keep us up late at night. We scribble our hopes and plans in the crinkled, coffee-stained margins of notebooks. We imagine all that could be. We can't help but share our excitement with others. We rejoice when someone else affirms or encourages us in that dream. Dreaming is fun and exciting!

So many people are scared to pursue a dream out of fear of failure, but for the brave ones who choose to move forward, there is often some sort of risk analysis that takes place in the dreamer's mind. Though she may not expect 100-percent success, the dreamer is hoping that her chance of a favorable outcome is higher than her chances of failure, for who wants to invest energy, hope, finances, and time into something that will not succeed? It's a mental commitment, and it's a giant step of faith with the desire for a happy ending. She plants the seed in her heart, and she tries her best to water it. She tends to it, prunes it as needed, and if the climate agrees, she fully expects to see it flourish. She's made all the preparations, so she thinks. But what the dreamer usually forgets to prepare for is the tendency she carries around in her heart to slowly and steadily elevate it above God's plan for her life. As the dreamer places her faith in the projected outcome and as she directs all her efforts to make this dream happen, she obsesses over the dream and becomes blind to any alternative ending to her story.

Let's face it, some of the greatest entrepreneurs of our time are where they are today because they gave themselves wholly to their mission. Steve Jobs saw a need, met that need, and created an empire. He envisioned his success, took a risk, gave it all he had, and now here I am typing on my Apple laptop next to my Apple iPhone. Entrepreneurs and creatives are cut from a different cloth, and they contribute so much to our daily living. We need innovative Christian men and women striving to do all things in excellence, boldly stepping out, and paving new paths in areas of technology, medicine, and so forth. However, when the outcome of our dream becomes our future hope, we have chosen to put our trust in the dream and not in God. When our whole world is tied to our dream—when we eat, sleep, and breathe for, say photography, or for moving up the corporate ladder, or for becoming a big deal in a certain circle, or for even building a well in Africa, we have chosen to live for the dream and not for God. Trusting in our dream as a source of happiness or fulfillment becomes a form of earthly salvation. The dream becomes the hope that we look forward to and build our life upon. We trust it to bring us contentment, peace, and prosperity. In other words, somewhere along the way, we went from chasing a dream to worshiping it. To *not* follow our dream would lump us in with the rest of traditional society who are also searching for similar benefits. This is idolizing a dream, and it is quite similar to those who worshiped the idols of old. G. K. Beale puts it this way:

> To commit ourselves to some part of the creation more than to the Creator is idolatry. And when we worship something in creation, we become like it, as spiritually lifeless and insensitive to God as a piece of wood, rock or stone. We become spiritually blind,

> deaf and dumb even though we have physical eyes and ears. If we commit ourselves to something that does not have God's Spirit, to that degree, we will be lacking the Spirit. We will be like ancient Israel.[3]

Though we may not carve statues of wood or fashion a god out of metal, the outcome of worshiping our dreams is equivalent: we become empty fools on the path to our own destruction.

A few years ago, we spent a family weekend at the beach. Like every trip before and since, my son, Kaiden, attempted to carve out his own little pool of water a few yards from the rolling waves before him. Digging a hole in the sand and filling it with water seems to be the universal goal of kids at the beach, and the result is almost always the same: either a wave envelopes it, or the little bit of water that does pool up eventually seeps back into the ground. However, that Friday he successfully dug deep and wide enough for the water to hold a while. Despite the giant ocean at their disposal, my kids preferred playing around in that little pool of stagnant water. Later that evening, we went out for dinner and then decided to check on the pool after we finished. It hadn't been two hours, and the water did not hold. The pool he had carved out was empty.

The Israelites throughout the Old Testament were a people whose idolatrous lifestyle was a lot like these tiny pools in the sand. Despite God's miraculous methods of rescuing them from their bondage in Egypt and His continued provision in their desert wandering, they forsook God and turned to other gods. Jeremiah 2:13 (ESV) says, "For my people have committed two evils: they have forsaken me, the fountain of living waters, and hewed out cisterns for themselves, broken cisterns that can hold no water."

Jeremiah wrote this to warn Israel of their wrongdoings and, therefore, God's impending judgment would soon come onto them. His description of the broken cisterns presents almost an oxymoron as this labor that they did to hew out containers for themselves resulted in nothing. Historically, living in the dry region of the Middle East makes water a precious commodity—one that whole tribes and villages based their geographic location on. In biblical times, if villages were not near water, they needed a substantially sized cistern or reservoir capable of transporting this life-giving substance to maintain their life and their future. This picture of hewing out cisterns describes the great lengths required to carve rock or carve into the earth. The idea was to carry water to the reservoir or allow it to collect rain for storage. But, like my son's sand pool at the beach, a broken cistern could not permanently hold water. The broken cisterns either dried up completely or turned to muck and mire. The water was dangerous and not worthy of drinking, their labor was in vain, and their efforts probably only made their thirst grow. The original audience of Jeremiah 2:13 was well-aware that attempting to fill a broken cistern is entirely foolish, and yet, this is the visual God gives us of His people at this time.

The emptiness of the broken cistern reflects the vanity of us humans trying to do things on our own without seeking God and His will for us. Like God's people in Jeremiah 2, we try to drink from our broken pots, only to find no water by the time our lips get to the cistern. The ironic part is that we complain to God that we don't understand why He will not allow us to drink from the pots of our own construction suited for our own desires. We build colander after colander and then blame God when the water slips through the cracks, wondering why we remain unsatisfied and thirsty. We scrape a tiny hole in the ground, one that will inevitably run out of water, when an ocean is right next to us. Meanwhile, the entire time He has the cistern that will never go dry or empty, yet we will not humble ourselves and ask Him for it. God is the fountain of living waters ready to give in abundance, and yet His people's (and our) ingratitude toward His kindness and deliberate rejection of worshiping Him alone resulted in an unquenchable thirst.

Through the prophet Jeremiah, God warns and pleads with the people of Israel to turn back to Him, because apart from Him is not only emptiness but wrath and destruction. The gods the Israelites created for themselves would not save them. Likewise, our attempts at loving anything more than God lead us to our own destruction and leave us feeling empty and angry at the very One who wishes to help us.

How relevant this is for us. A 2020 cistern for a young woman may look less like worshiping a rain god and more like building her life upon an Instagram following. Perhaps she spends her days consumed with crafting the right feed and obsessing over her number of followers, likes, and comments. Or maybe her worth is found in her career, achievements, marriage, friendships, kids, influence, appearance, or zip code. Even these good things can become distorted. The bottom line is: if God isn't our first love, then something or someone else is. Consider this thought by Pastor John Piper:

> If you could have heaven, with no sickness, and with all the friends you ever had on earth, and all the food you ever liked, and all the leisure activities you ever enjoyed, and all the natural beauties you ever saw, all the physical pleasures you ever tasted, and no human conflict or any natural disasters, could you be satisfied with heaven, if Christ were not there?[4]

I first heard this question in high school. I knew the Sunday school answer: no, of course not. But deep within I felt convicted that I could have answered yes, I might be okay. An eternity with no sickness and all the comforts I longed for sounded incredible. I could feel complete if all my friends and family and loved ones were there. It scared me that I might be satisfied with a life apart from God. This vision of Utopia within my mind had me—not God—as its center, and these honest thoughts revealed that I didn't have a genuine love for God.

But what I've learned over the years is this: heaven is not heaven apart from God. God is the source of all goodness, and if we were to remove that Source, we would be in hell. Therefore, this theoretical model of heaven will not produce an ounce of happiness apart from God's presence.

Any blessing on earth that I take pleasure in: love, creative endeavors, even the very sun shining on my face, may be enjoyed to a certain degree apart from God because of common grace. The definition of common grace is "the grace of God by which He gives people innumerable blessings that are not part of salvation. The word *common* here means something that is common to all people and is not restricted to believers or to the elect only."[5] This means that the person who rejects God can still enjoy certain graces here upon earth, albeit temporarily.

Brad Evangelista, a former pastor of ours from our church in Georgia, would often give this sort of an illustration for common grace: a non-Christian can enjoy the same steak that I'm eating. He or she can appreciate the taste, texture, and flavor. That is common grace. And yet, they cannot enjoy it the way God intended them to because they eat it while rejecting the God who graciously gave them that steak. They cannot take a bite and rejoice in God for creating this steak, blessing them with this steak, and giving them the health to eat this steak. For the non-Christian, it's simply a carnal, fleeting pleasure. Christians enjoy eating in a totally different manner because we recognize that there's a God behind all the complexity of life, even the various flavors at play in our food. We experience everything as an extension of His creativity and care for us. We can worship Him in everything we do—even eating! And we know that this very God is the One who we were once separated from, if it weren't for Christ. Our salvation in Him makes us burst in gratitude for all the good He gives us (especially the flavorful kinds of good in this life). My point is that one can reach the highest heights of fame and fortune, appear to have absolutely no need of God, and claim to be quite "happy," but her form of happiness is fractured, corrupted, and is not even an iota of what true biblical happiness or blessedness is. Her experience of every created thing is divorced from the One who created it.

So, let's rework Piper's question to fit our context: If you could have a life with every dream fulfilled and every goal of yours met, would you be satisfied if God were not a part of it? If you had that Instagram following, that level of fame, that certain relationship, that security of knowing your kids are okay, that perfect body, that standing ovation from your company, that alleviation from suffering, or that number in the bank account, but Jesus was a stranger to you, would you really care? Would you be fulfilled? There may be "happiness" for a season, but the answer is no. If we are truly God's elect, then there is no satisfaction in anything, no matter how good, apart from Him. Or here's another question to test our devotion to God: If you could die right now and be with God, would you want to? Many would say, "Well yes, but I hope I can get married first," or "I hope I can reach my goals first." The heart of these questions is simple: Do we love God? Or do we love the dreams that we have for ourselves more?

Dreams in Proper Perspective

Hannah of 1 Samuel was a woman with a clear dream: she wanted a child. Unlike much of popular culture today, a child was not a hindrance to a woman's dream for herself. Today children are often viewed as inconvenient, life-sucking beings that hold us back from living our best lives now. I cannot tell you how many times I've walked through a store with my three kids only to hear a random commentator say, "I remember those days . . ." The warm smile deceives me, and just as I think she will reflect on a fond memory of some sort, the bystander continues, "I don't miss it one bit. I'm so glad my children are grown up and out of the house." Yes, not every shopping trip is easy, but as a whole, I have no desire to wish this part of my life away. The bystander offers comfort in the form of the future hope that someday your kids will leave you and you can be on your own again, where life isn't inconvenient anymore and you no longer have to invest in the hard ways. *You'll get to the place where you can just do you,* in other words. While yes, parenting is hard, and there are days we need rest and help, comments like these reinforce the idea that life is really about us in the end, as long as we just do our part now. In our culture, the beautiful and God-given role of parenting—or really, our commitment to *any* sort of opportunity to live the gospel daily—is exchanged for a lie that says our time is better spent elsewhere.

But in biblical times? The child was the dream. One primary example is the covenant between God and Abram found in Genesis 13:15–16 where God's ultimate blessing was the gift of "offspring." Psalm 127:4–5a says, "Like arrows in the hand of a warrior are the sons born in one's youth. Happy is the man who has filled his quiver with them." Children were an inheritance from the Lord. They were a visible display of God's blessing. And on top of that, they were a source of security for the future. Having kids meant survival—it meant having hands to work in the family business and in the fields so everyone could eat, and it meant having someone to take care of you in old age. Kids weren't accessories. They were necessities, and having many of them made a woman highly esteemed in her circles. Being around a woman with lots of kids meant being around that girl who got the dream.

It's no wonder that so many women in the pages of Scripture before Hannah—Sarah, wife of Abraham; Rebekah, wife of Isaac; Rachel, wife of Jacob; the unnamed wife of Manoah (or Samson's mom)—shared in the same anguish of Hannah, as she was barren and unable to conceive. Her circumstances were doubly distressing as she was wife number one of two. It's presumed that Elkanah, her husband, married his second wife, Peninnah, because Hannah could not bear children. Unfortunately, his other wife wasn't a sweet woman of compassion to Hannah. Scripture says that Peninnah would "taunt her severely just to provoke her, because the LORD had kept Hannah from conceiving" (1 Sam. 1:6). Think about that thing you desire, that dream you just can't stop fixating on, and now imagine your rival—that girl who has accomplished what you long for—barraging you on the regular, rubbing it in your face.

Poor Hannah wrestled with much vexation and torment, but Scripture makes it clear that she carried herself with grace and godliness. Hannah didn't allow her very real and valid emotions to turn into a pity party. Throughout her story, we read that she remained respectful to her husband, full of humility, and filled with hope and trust in the Lord. She could have quickly become bitter and acted in retaliation to Peninnah. She could have grown resentful to Elkanah for marrying a cruel woman. She could have grown in bitterness to God for closing her womb.

But we don't see Hannah doing any of that. She did not gather with other wives and gossip about Peninnah to make herself feel better or throw herself into the arms of her husband for comfort, trying to win his affection or prove that she was the better choice. In short, Hannah did not try to find her satisfaction in temporary things. No, her distress directed her to pray. Deeply wounded from Penninah's attacks and grappling with her real longing for a child, Hannah prayed to the Lord. With tears streaming down her face, she pleaded with the Lord and vowed, "Lord of Armies, if you will take notice of your servant's affliction, remember and not forget me, and give your servant a son, I will give him to the LORD all the days of his life, and his hair will never be cut" (1 Sam. 1:11). Hannah went straight to the Source—the One who speaks and life is created (Gen. 1). The One who makes us in His image (Gen. 1:27). The One who supplies us breath (Isa. 42:5). But she didn't make a request for her own personal benefit. She vowed her child to His service and boldly declared that she would give her son in service to the Lord "all the days of his life."

We've all seen those movies, the ones where the fictional character doesn't believe in God but talks to Him anyway saying, "If you get me out of this situation, I won't ever (fill in the blank) again." Hannah's prayer wasn't a desperate proclamation made in a near-death situation. Given her character and her state while praying, we can surmise that this prayer was not Hannah's way of trying to twist God's arm. It was a sincere, straight-from-the-heart, I'm-wholly-trusting-in-God vow. And in God's perfect timing and according to His perfect purposes, He answers her prayer. In chapter 2, He opens her womb and gives her Samuel.

Most striking about this is from Hannah's vantage point, she was praying for a child. But from God's vantage point, His purpose in answering her prayer went far beyond allowing her to be a mother. He had a plan for the nation of Israel through Samuel which connected to His plan for the world through Jesus Christ. We can take heart in that for our own lives. God is directing every detail in our circumstances, and His plans are always so much bigger than our own.

Hannah honored her vow and as soon as she was done nursing, she brought sacrifices for her and Elkanah to offer, as well as her precious boy Samuel to be given up for lifelong ministry.

The question I had when studying Hannah is what kind of a woman—tormented for years over her inability to have a child—would ask for a child and then immediately commit that child to the Lord for the entirety of his life? The answer is the kind of woman who was wholly devoted to the Lord. Her identity was secure in God.

Just moments before her bold vow, Elkanah asked her, "Am I not better to you than ten sons?" (v. 8). He saw her distress and was simply trying to help. He was basically saying, "Isn't our marriage enough? Can't I satisfy?" He was kind to her. He loved her. He was aware of her hurt and made efforts to alleviate the situation (like putting a double portion of food on her plate at the feast) (v. 5). Hannah could have easily found temporary comfort in her husband. Isn't this our natural tendency? We long for something, and when we don't get it, we try to make ourselves feel better with something that just as much won't satisfy as God will? We hit the gym. We get our hair done. We go on that shopping spree, rent that movie, indulge in that chocolate cake, and read the self-help book to empower ourselves. In the name of transparency, we post about our lack and try to make the comments and likes fill the empty space. But all of this can only fill us up to a certain point. Our bodies lose their shape. Our highlights grow out. The film turns out to be a flop. Our satisfaction for the cake disappears as fast as the next meal comes. All of the ways the world tries to Band-Aid the pain will not fix the root problem because we were made to be satisfied by God alone.

Hannah's identity was not found in her marriage. It was not found in her social status or approval amongst friends (or in this case, other wives). And if you read the entirety of chapter 2, it is clear that her identity was not found in her being a mother. Why? Because before she even has her son, she commits him to the Lord. When she finally has him, she gives him back to the Lord. And when she prays a prayer of gratitude after dropping Samuel off at the temple in chapter 2, not once does she mention her son in her prayer of gratitude to God; her entire prayer is simply about God. "There is no one holy like the LORD. There is no one besides you! And there is no rock like our God" (1 Sam. 2:2). On and on she goes praising the Lord, proclaiming His goodness to all the people. One commentator tells us exactly what made Hannah's prayer so remarkable:

> We note that Hannah draws on the vocabulary of Israel's history. Hannah sounds like a victorious army because she was echoing the language of Israel on occasions of great deliverance by God. In particular, she seems to express the same sentiments as Moses and the people of Israel after they were rescued from the Egyptians . . . We might describe the body of Hannah's prayer as a Biblical worldview. This is what the world looks like when your heart exults in the Lord and you rejoice in his salvation . . .

> Human power and human weakness look completely different if you believe in God as Hannah believed in God.[6]

Hannah had a proper perspective of God and, therefore, her identity remained rooted in God—not her husband, or other women's estimation of her, or the hope of a child, or the child himself when he did arrive. She could have easily idolized motherhood, but her understanding of God was greater than her dream to be a mother. Yes, she had the dream of being a mother. She didn't hide her tears or act like the dream wasn't there. But instead of making that dream god, she gave it to God, because He mattered more to her than her ache for a baby, real and palpable as it was. She placed her hope, her life, her identity wholly in Him alone, and all of His kindness was affirmed when He chose to answer her prayer. Hannah is a model of godliness we ought to pattern our lives and our dreaming after.

What Drives Us?

My husband and I lead a young adult's group at our church, and one question he asks regularly is: *Why do you wake up each morning? What drives you to make it through another day?* Our response to this question tells us a lot about our goals and priorities in life. My desire to become a successful photographer was the reason I woke up each morning. I chased after the next "dream wedding" that would land me a blog feature, give me more status/credibility as an artist, and increase my bookings. For others, the motivation for why they do all that they do could be working out, looking into the mirror, and seeing a flawless body that looks good in any outfit. It may not be photography or body image for every person, but if we are honest with ourselves, we all have something that we are tempted to put on the throne that belongs only to God. These idols may be the reason we continue to make our decisions and plan our futures off of a potentiality that could very well not come true. The reality is that regardless of whether or not it does or does not come true, our dream will not satisfy us the way that God will. We must ask God to help us identify and remove the things that we have placed on His rightful throne of our hearts.

I am not saying that we cannot have goals and ambition. I'm not saying that we cannot plan for the future, but the key to these things is what Solomon wrote in Proverbs 16:9: "A person's heart plans his way, but the LORD determines his steps." I am a planner, and I like to do things my way. But as I grow older and experience more of life, I've come to recognize that not every plan of mine will pan out the way I hope, and that is okay because I can trust that God is laying a better path before me and directing my steps.

Rather than treating Him like a genie, we need to treat Him with the love, honor, and respect He is more than worthy of. We must remember that He's far better than a genie who will grant us some wishes if we ask the right way—He's a Father whose arm can't be twisted or manipulated, who loves us regardless of our performance, who gives us what we need when we can't see that we need it. In all our dreaming, we must seek His will for our lives and ask that He grant us the spiritual sensitivity to identify a clear direction for the complex decisions we face. Like Hannah, we must simply continue to honor and worship God above all our desires, and trust Him when we do not know the outcome on the other side of our asking.

But here's the great news in all of this. We actually do know the outcome of our lives if we are in Christ. All of the things I desire will be mine in Christ through Christ at the end of the age. This is what it means to "delight in the LORD, and He will give you the desires of your heart" (Ps. 37:4). As we delight in Him through the hallowing of His name and the seeking of His will, our desires align with God's. As we conform to His image, we will naturally want what He wants. This relieves the pressure we put on ourselves to follow a worldly standard for our best lives now and results in proper worship of God as the

Holy Sovereign Creator, not as the genie in the sky we hope will give us what we want.

For those who read this and think, "I don't know that I can love a God who may not fulfill my dream," we must ask ourselves, "Do I truly love God? Am I truly a Christian?" I know that this is a bold and blunt question to throw out here, but self-examination is scriptural. Paul concludes his letter to the Corinthians with this: "Test yourselves to see if you are in the faith. Examine yourselves. Or do you yourselves not recognize that Jesus Christ is in you?—unless you fail the test" (2 Cor. 13:5). Just as my high school English teacher asked me to examine my heart, he challenges his readers to make sure that they are actually in Christ and not self-deceived, like I was prior to my conversion in high school.

C. H. Spurgeon addresses this topic and says, "Many have been lost and are wailing at their everlasting ruin. Their loss is to be traced to nothing more than that they never examined themselves to discover whether they were in the faith. We are to test and examine ourselves because God will examine us."[7] Pursuing our own will above God's will, idolizing a dream, and not knowing God are eternal matters with life-and-death consequences. We must be 100-percent sure that we aren't fooling ourselves because inheriting the kingdom of God is what is at stake. Our life right now echoes into eternity, and we must keep this mind-set so we can share in proper communion with Christ.

The question I had to ask myself all those years ago, and the question I ask of you today is this: Do you know God? I don't mean do you know about God, but do you personally know God? Do you truly have a heart (not just some mental answers) for spiritual things? Or have the lies of the world affected you so much that you care more about building your kingdom here rather than seeking God's kingdom? Can you say that you are trusting in Him (and, therefore, the plan He has written for your life)?

While having a dream isn't necessarily wrong, we need to decide which of these two options we will choose when pursuing one: we can either cling to the dream or cling to God. We can thirst at the broken well or we can drink from the living water. Both require our total devotion, but only one leads to true blessedness.

Chapter 3

DOES DYING TO SELF MEAN DYING TO OUR DREAMS?

"Are all things . . . held loosely, ready to be parted with without a struggle when He asks for them?"[1]

—I. Lilias Trotter

Ethan and I spent our first anniversary in Hawaii. While he surfed the glassy, reef-filled waters, I curled up with a book on the shoreline a few hundred feet from him. I couldn't have asked for a more picturesque setting. The problem was that I could not manage to stay awake to actually enjoy it. I felt so sleepy and fought the urge to nap. The thought of snoozing on the beach scared me. I had my expensive camera gear alongside me and feared both the beach thief and the sneak attack of a wave. "I'm just going to go to the hotel and take a nap. I think all this sun is making me sleepy," I told Ethan as he came up to grab a drink of water. I went back to the hotel room, opened the screen door, and exchanged the cold AC hotel air for the warm, salty Hawaiian breeze. The sound of rolling waves in the background lulled me to sleep in no time.

I woke up four hours later! Go figure, Ethan was still surfing and hadn't even noticed. When we reunited for dinner, we joked about how he flew to Hawaii to surf, and I flew to Hawaii to nap.

After we arrived back in California and adjusted to our normal routine, I was shocked that I still lacked energy. I was in a constant state of sleepiness, and no amount of coffee kept me from napping all the time. I'm not sure what led us to go out and buy a pregnancy test, but we did, and on April 1, 2010 (that's right—April Fool's Day!), I found out I was pregnant. In a matter of minutes, my entire world changed. "This is an April Fool's joke, right? I can't imagine the responsibility of a child at twenty-one years old. I didn't expect to be a mom this early in life." While I knew this child was a gift from God, growing our family this early into our marriage was not on our radar. I wanted some time to get to know Ethan better, explore California a bit more, and give my full attention to my photography business. I knew my response was selfish, but for an overly tired twenty-one-year-old newlywed, I had some serious emotions to process. All my plans, hopes, and dreams had come to a screeching halt.

Death to a Dream

I truly believe that God allows a woman to carry a life in her womb for nine months for far more than developmental reasons. Regardless of whether a woman is planning or not, there is mental preparation for what is to come. God used the next several months to refine me and rid me of the self-centered, ugliness of my own heart. There were days where I was incredibly excited at the thought of holding a little one, and there were days I was engulfed by fear. Motherhood, among many things, is most definitely a tool for sanctification, and as my son Kaiden grew within me, so did my love for this little boy. The more I felt Kai's presence through little kicks, the more I embraced the new role I would step into within our growing family. Moreover, the best part about it was that photography remained something that I could do on the weekends while being a stay-at-home mom for my babe.

Kaiden was born in November, which felt like perfect timing for me because my wedding season had come to a close. Those first few months were a mixture of hardship and sweetness as Ethan and I learned so much about ourselves and each other in our sleep-deprived state. By springtime, I booked only a few weddings for that year. I decided to seek out second shooter opportunities to build my portfolio and assist primary photographers at their client's wedding. I sent out at least a dozen e-mails to well-established photographers from all over the Bay Area whose work I admired. I hadn't heard anything for about two weeks and impatiently assumed that the lack of response was a sign that God did not want my business to head in that direction.

However, it was not long after reaching that conclusion that a photographer named Jared sent me a Facebook message. His message said, "I need a second shooter this summer for weddings. If you're interested, I would love to set up a meeting." But then there was a separate message that immediately followed: "I don't know what's up with Facebook, but as soon as I sent that message to you, it delivered your message to me apparently from April 8th. So sorry for not responding—but I didn't even know you had written to me." In short, I had written to him on April 8, but he didn't see that message until after he wrote to me on April 21. We both found it incredibly strange that he had reached out to me not knowing that I had reached out to him. The best part was that we were both Christians. He was an older gentleman, married with children, and served as a part-time worship pastor at his church. Jared not only became a photography mentor for me, but a friend. Working with him gave me the opportunity to photograph all the glamorous weddings that I had spent so much time dreaming of while avoiding the incredible amount of pressure that the primary shooter faces.

I strengthened my skills under his mentorship. We photographed at a variety of fancy California hotels, vineyards, and beautiful backyard weddings. I felt the highs of capturing some near perfect shots and the lows when I would fail to capture an important moment well or when I would compare my work to Jared's. As he gave me more responsibility, the stress and burden I placed on myself to make sure

I represented his brand well continued to grow. All the while, I felt increasing frustration and confusion about my own photography business. I wrestled with the fact that the art form I loved had turned into stressful work that I dreaded. By the end of the season, I concluded that I did not love wedding photography the way I thought I did. God had done it—He had given me exactly what I wanted through the form of second shooting, and I realized I didn't want it after all. It didn't fulfill me the way I had hoped.

I envisioned a career in photography like climbing a ladder. Here I was, striving to rise higher and higher, trying to reach the same heights, if not higher, than some of my favorite photographers. I was so focused on gripping one rail to the next that I hadn't considered looking up and seeing those photographers who may not feel they have attained the height of their career just yet. Who was it that they, like me, looked up to and idolized, creating a sense of discontent with their own current position? I thought about the fact that even the most talented of photographers will probably never take a picture that would lead them to say, "That was the best shot of my life. I am content and never need to take a photo again." Whether it's photography or any other type of dream, the ladder of "success" never ends.

As I reflected on this more, I realized that even if I achieved all the successes my heart had hoped for, apart from an active relationship with God, I would always remain empty. If I was not content with the life He had given me now, how could I expect to be satisfied with the life I dreamed of? I had the head knowledge that there is no lasting hope in photography, and yet for a long time I didn't apply that knowledge to my living. The calling to walk away from this dream job continued to grow with every passage of Scripture I read, every sermon preached at church, and even comments by officiators made at some of the Christian weddings I photographed. Photography itself wasn't the problem—the hope I had placed in it, and the obsession I had created over it was. While I was scared to let go of this chapter in my life, I knew that the unknown outcome of obedience would be far greater than what lay ahead had I continued forcing my dream. Though God sometimes calls us to stay the course in situations like these, and though some may be called to work outside the home in various seasons of their life, I knew that for me, in this season and situation, God was calling me to lay this dream down. My situation was simple—I had fashioned an idol, and God was calling me to leave it, just as He did with plenty of people in Scripture. I didn't know if that meant I'd ever return to photography or if the Lord had other plans in store, but I did know idolatry wasn't okay, and I simply needed to obey God's prompting and trust Him. So, I laid down my dream. I finished up my commitments and desired to wholeheartedly refocus on my relationship with God and care for my family and home.

Saul on a Mission

The story of Paul's life is an incredible example of someone's life trajectory completely changing courses. We already talked about him and his writing a little so far, but let us examine him more closely and consider who he was, what impact the gospel made on his own life, and the result of his changed life. Here are the facts we know about Paul:

1. We know that Paul was also named Saul. One was his Roman name, the other his Jewish name. (You will find that I go between these two names often. They are the same person.)
2. He was born in Tarsus, and his proud Jewish lineage is traced back to the tribe of Benjamin (Phil. 3:5). He was also a Roman citizen (Acts 22:28), a tentmaker by trade (Acts 18:3), and a Pharisee like his father (Phil. 3:5).

3. At a young age, he studied under Gamaliel, a leading authority at that time in Jewish culture (Acts 22:3), and Galatians 1:14 tells us that he excelled among his peers in his studies. This means he grew up with a rich understanding of Old Testament history, in addition to his rabbinical education.

Saul's citizenship may have given him nobility, but his earned title of Pharisee set him apart from modern-day Jews. The name Pharisee can be interpreted to mean "loyal to God."[2] Everything from a Pharisee's strict adherence to the Law to their distinguished apparel reflected a status of prominence amongst other Jewish men of his day. One of the primary roles of a Pharisee was to interpret Scripture to bring other followers of God into conformity for holy living. Pharisees were elitists in the context of religion, and the ever-increasing paganism around them only fueled their desire to cling to tradition and nationalism.

Though they awaited the Messiah, their hardness of heart and blindness kept more of them from recognizing Jesus to be the only "name under heaven given to people by which we must be saved" (Acts 4:12). The book of Matthew contains the longest discourse between Jesus and the Pharisees. Jesus rebukes them, "For they preach, but do not practice . . . they do all their deeds to be seen by others . . . you shut the kingdom of heaven in people's faces" (23:3–5, 13 ESV). This was possibly some of the most shocking criticism they had heard in their lifetime. Jesus continues: "Snakes! Brood of vipers! How can you escape being condemned to hell?" (Matt. 23:33). Over and over again Jesus refers to these law-keepers as blind, guiding people in the ways of outward cleanliness but completely neglecting the rotting corpse inside of themselves.

Put yourself in the Pharisees' sandals. You're in a culture completely cut off from anything unclean or unholy around you. You're striving to be the best of the best amongst a group of others striving to do the same. Your whole existence centers around what you think is pleasing to God. You are committed to never letting what happened in your people's history—namely, rebellion against God by not keeping his Law—happen again. So you police everybody. This was clearly a breeding ground for pride. (Talk about being self-deceived.) And now you have some guy claiming to be the Messiah telling you who have worked so hard at keeping the Mosaic and Levitical law[3] that your deeds are worthless and not heaven-worthy? God's people went through countless cycles of not obeying the Law, and now you're here, whipping these sinners into shape so that no one does that again. *Who in the world does this carpenter think he is, saying that your work is shutting people out of heaven?* Your entire reason for monitoring everyone's law-keeping is precisely the opposite! You're trying to make sure everyone does get to stay in God's good graces. The Law is how God is pleased, right? It's how we get to enjoy His presence. *This rebel rabbi doesn't know what he's talking about—he's clearly just stirring up trouble and leading the people astray, just as they've been led away from the Law before!* Not believing that Jesus is the Messiah, I can see why they must have felt pure rage toward Him.

With that background in mind, Acts introduces us to Saul in his early years. This period in time was after Jesus' death where Saul stands as a witness to the stoning of Stephen. Stephen was a disciple arrested for proclaiming the gospel and performing signs and wonders. A group of instigators riled the crowd and falsely accused Stephen of speaking against Moses and God. Stephen stood before all the senate of Israel, also known as the Sanhedrin, and with what Scripture describes as having "the face of an angel" (recognized by all who sat in the council—Saul included), Stephen began to address the faults of the council, reciting Old Testament history, pointing out Israel's waywardness, and revealing Israel's present rejection of the Messiah. This council had worked hard to eliminate the rapidly growing early church, and Stephen represented one more faithful follower of Jesus they needed to make an example of.

It's an interesting thought that Saul was right there, listening to Stephen's speech as Stephen spoke filled with the Holy Spirit. Despite the truth declared before all, Saul stood in approval of execution as the witnesses laid down their garments so they could stone Stephen to death (Acts 7:58). And with the same fervent zeal that motivated Saul's studies in his youth, he went out of his way to continue attacking Christians by requesting permission to ravage the early church, one house at a time. Saul sparked a season of persecution, holding nothing back as he dragged men and women off to prison. The threat for the early church saints moved from city to city and Stephen's persecution caused many to disperse and flee to other cities. It would take divine intervention to reach a heart as cold as Saul's.

Saul truly thought that he was doing the Lord's work. He dedicated his life to studying the traditions and laws and wished to earn a right standing before his Creator. In so doing, he thought that by purging followers of Christ he was purging a perverted form of Judaism. Remember, God's people had followed after false beliefs and teachers before. To prevent this, Saul performed tasks and rituals that he thought would spare the people from straying and earn him a seat in heaven, when in reality his trajectory would land him a seat in hell. Saul was not out seeking the Lord's will; he assumed it. As we read the story, we can clearly see that Saul didn't pray to God asking Him what is it that He wished for Saul to do or what path to take that would be pleasing to God. Instead, Saul followed the religious leaders and traditions of his day. He trusted that his desires, his prior knowledge, his passion and zeal, his natural knack for understanding the finer points of Jewish theology, the permission he was granted to go ahead from his human authority and peers, and his plans were right. He sought no counsel from God and pursued what was right in his own eyes.

Similarly, I assumed that wedding photography was God's plan for my life. I had a natural knack for it, I had knowledge about it, I had passion and zeal for it, and my peers and even those I deemed photography "authorities" were giving me the green light. With all these "yeses" around me, I simply assumed God was orchestrating them all, and that He was guiding me toward my photographic destiny. But the truth was, I wasn't really engaging with *Him* over it. It's all too easy to assume something is right and proper in our lives and consider everyone else's input on the matter, yet fail to seek God's leading in our decision making. It's true, God knows our thoughts and deeds, but we are still called to engage with Him, to seek His will, or as Colossians 1:9–14 says, "be filled with the knowledge of his will."

Definitions Matter

What is the gospel? Define it. I posed this question to the ladies in my small group at our midweek Bible study. Many of our small group questions referred to the gospel during our opening lesson, so I felt that this was a fundamental question to ask, especially considering how much Scripture emphasizes the preaching of the true gospel. Galatians 1:6–8 (emphasis mine) says,

> I am amazed that you are so quickly turning away from him who called you by the grace of Christ and *are turning to a different gospel—not that there is another gospel*, but there are some who are troubling you and want to *distort the gospel of Christ*. But even if we or an angel from heaven should preach to you *a gospel contrary to what we have preached to you*, a curse be on him! As we have said before, I now say again: If anyone is preaching to you *a gospel contrary to what you received,* a curse be on him!

This is a very interesting (and stark!) greeting Paul gives to the church in Galatia, but can be taken as a warning for us in our modern day. Clearly this church was plagued by false teachers who distorted the truth and the very essence of the gospel message, but the people within this church were unable to recognize forgery from the truth. This is the very distortion of sound doctrine that we talked about in chapter 1 and, unfortunately, we see this in our day—especially in the space of Christian dreamers.

The writer in Hebrews 2 describes this as a slow drift away from the truth. This drift is similar to what someone experiences when she ventures out into the ocean in a boat without setting an anchor to keep her position firmly planted near the shore. Before she knows it, she will drift miles away from the safety of land, without any inkling of the danger she is in. She'll hear the lapping waves around her, exotic and calming, and she'll be lulled out of alertness, unaware of the creatures and currents beneath the water, and the scorching hot sun above—all of which will eventually kill her if she doesn't snap out of it and get back to land. So, we must be sure that we have a firm understanding on the "what" of the gospel—it's our anchor, our assurance of safe and dry land. Without the gospel as our anchor, we'll drift out into nonsense that sounds exotic or nice, but pulls us toward a sure path to death.

When it comes to knowing what's right, we must have something to compare it to outside of our own opinion, lest we become like Saul and think that what we *feel* or *assume* is gospel-truth. Also, knowing exactly what the "good news" is will give us wisdom so we can ensure we are not like the members of the church in Galatia if we come across someone teaching, preaching, or even writing a different gospel other than what is found in the Scriptures. Additionally, it will directly impact the way we live and, therefore, the way we dream. The gospel is defined by the Bible. False gospels (which include certain messages about chasing our dreams) are not. So anytime we want to know if the "good news" we are hearing is actually correct—whether we hear that message in a conversation, on social media, on a podcast, or otherwise—we need to compare it to what the Bible has to say.

After I posed the question to my small group, there was a long pause of silence. Answering questions in small group can be awkward, and on top of that, I'm sure the fact that it was not on our discussion guide caught them off guard. I didn't bring it up to embarrass or discourage them; rather, I wanted to get their minds engaged to think about the very phrase we hear, say, and read pretty often. One brave woman spoke up and answered correctly, but the time it took to hear a response from any of the ladies made me think—*Shouldn't this message roll off our tongues? Don't we center our whole life around believing and sharing this good news?* Out of all the things we could talk about (and if you're anything like me, I can be quite chatty), is this not the one message we are supposed to communicate regularly and confidently?

Because the message of salvation directly affects our souls both now (in the ways we approach our entire lives) and in eternal life to come (in heaven or hell)—it is of utmost importance that our definition of the gospel be clear. If faith comes by hearing the message of Christ, we better make sure we get it right (Rom. 10:17). If we don't, we'll end up like the girl drifting off into a nebulous oblivion where the swarming sharks and the scorching sun await us.

The gospel means "good news," and there is so much truth packed into these two words that it may be a Christian's tendency to grow lazy and rely upon this two-word summary. Others may be intimidated at the thought of explaining the gospel message. Thinking about sin, sacrifices, and Jesus' life, death, and resurrection overwhelm them, and they avoid any opportunities to share because they don't fully know how to verbalize it. I encourage you to take a moment and write down your own definition of the gospel before you continue reading. Maybe this is a no-brainer for you, but for others, this may be a bit of a challenge. Exercise your mind a little and think it through—what all is packaged into the two little words: *the gospel*? If someone asked you about it right now, how would you explain it?

The Gospel Defined

As we define the gospel, let's start from the beginning. And stick with me—understanding the whole story of God's historical redemption matters a great deal to the topic of dream-chasing as a Christian.

God created mankind to love, serve, and obey Him, and to flourish in their relationship with one another and with creation. Before Adam and Eve sinned, humanity was in perfect relationship with God and the world. They enjoyed the presence of God, and they lived to glorify Him alone in all their endeavors. Remember the garden scene in Genesis where Satan deceived Adam and Eve? Desiring to be like God, Adam and Eve rebelled against God's commandments and ate the forbidden fruit. They acted independently of God, and the single sin that they were assured would make them like God turned out to do the exact opposite. Their sin separated them from God who is holy, and their exile from the garden drove them away from His presence. They were spiritually dead, now in the process of physically dying (not an immediate death but rather facing the curse of death), bearing a sinful nature, and were absolutely nothing like God.

This portion of biblical history is often referred to as "the Fall." It is here we see one foundational truth of the gospel which is that all of humanity is born with a sinful nature, thereby separating us from a holy God (Isa. 53:6). J. I. Packer defines sin as, "rebellion against God's rule, missing the mark God set us to aim at, transgressing God's law, disobeying God's directives, offending God's purity by defiling oneself, and incurring guilt before God the Judge . . . Sin may comprehensively defined as lack of conformity to the law of God in act, habit, attitude, outlook, disposition, motivation, and mode of existence."[4] Sin is in direct rebellion and opposition to God, and all of mankind will have to answer for it, for not one of us is perfectly righteous or without sin (Rom. 3:9–12, 23). No one human being in his or her strength can do anything to show worthiness or merit before the Lord. In fact, not only are we unable to merit God's favor in our own strength, the Bible actually says we are *dead* in our trespasses (Eph. 2:1–2). A dead person can't save herself. The Bible also uses another word for our relationship to sin: we are *slaves* to it (John 8:34). We cannot choose another way. Because of this, we are considered God's enemy, and without Christ to absorb it for us, wrath for our sins await us (Rom. 5:10; Eph. 2:3). So, for anyone who thinks they are outside of these truths, 1 John 1:8 calls this person out: "If we say, 'We have no sin,' we are deceiving ourselves, and the truth is not in us."

Life outside of the garden was significantly different from God's original design. Throughout Genesis and early chapters in Exodus, we read the consequences of a sin-filled world. By Exodus 20, God provides a standard of living for His people through the Ten Commandments. God literally set His law in stone, which outlined the parameters for daily living. Now there could be no arguing about whether or not murder was wrong or if multiple gods was acceptable worship. Not only did the law make us conscious of our sin (Rom. 3:20), it also set His people apart from the rest of the world. When Jesus answers what the first greatest commandment is (as found in Matthew 22), He repeats what was commanded in Deuteronomy 6:5: "Love the Lord your God with all your heart, with all your soul, and with all your strength." This encompassed the first four of the Ten Commandments that are vertical in nature as it concerns our relationship with God. Jesus continues this by adding, "Love your neighbor as yourself" (Matt. 22:39), which demonstrates the last six commandments to be lived out horizontally in how Christians are to interact with those around us. Loving God and loving our neighbors is the common denominator of the law. Something important to note is that even under the old law, God has always desired a heart in devotion to Him and not merely a rule follower. Whether following the old law or entering into the New Covenant, He wants us to love and obey Him above all things.

The law was a good gift to God's people, but here's the thing—even as God was speaking the law for Moses to record, Israel was in the process of breaking it! While Moses was on top of Mount Sinai, the Israelites waited impatiently at the bottom of the mountain creating a golden calf to worship. Their behavior foreshadowed their future behavior, which displays just how much they would need an intercessor between God and man. And so God instituted the Levitical priesthood to mediate between the two.

These priests had specific requirements that ranged from what kind of clothing they could wear to how they should approach the tabernacle. This task was not something one would take lightly as even the slightest error would result in their death. The primary responsibility of the priest was to handle the substitutionary sacrifice. This priest would enter the tabernacle once a year and offer a sacrifice on behalf of the transgressor. Hebrews 9:22 says, "According to the law almost everything is purified with blood, and without the shedding of blood there is no forgiveness." Once the sins of the people had been paid for, their standing with God was restored once again.

This theme of forsaking God and putting their trust in man-made sources is repeated throughout all the Old Testament as the people of Israel continually broke His law over and over again, and their transgressions had to likewise be paid for repetitively. James 2:10 declares: "For whoever keeps the entire law, and yet stumbles at one point, is guilty of breaking it all." They struggled to follow the law perfectly, and there wasn't a single person able to keep the whole law. Every lamb offered as a sacrifice foreshadowed the Lamb of God that was to come.

But none of this was a surprise to God. He provided a plan of redemption for all mankind in a promise He made to Eve in Genesis 3:15, where God tells her that out of her lineage a Savior is coming who will crush the head of Satan. That Savior is Jesus; He is the solution:

> But Christ has appeared as a *high priest* of the good things that have come. In the *greater and more perfect*

> *tabernacle* not made with hands (that is, not of this creation), he entered the most holy place once for all time, not by the blood of goats and calves, but *by his own blood*, having obtained eternal redemption. For if the blood of goats and bulls and the ashes of a young cow, sprinkling those who are defiled, sanctify for the purification of the flesh, how much more will the blood of Christ, who through the eternal Spirit offered himself without blemish to God, cleanse our consciences from dead works so that we can serve the living God?
>
> Therefore, he is the mediator of a new covenant, so that those who are called might receive the promise of the eternal inheritance, because a death has taken place for redemption from the transgressions committed under the first covenant. (Heb. 9:11–15, emphasis mine)

Jesus is the High Priest and the better tabernacle! He is the spotless Lamb and the new mediator or intercessor! Jesus is God's ultimate sacrifice to free His people from turning to the "copies" or "shadows" they would perform day after day and year after year (Heb. 10:1) Even if the priests offered sacrifices repeatedly for all of eternity, their atonement could never take away the sins of the world. The very fact that the sacrifices had to be repeated over and over again only proves that they weren't sufficient. The sin outdid the sacrifice every time. Yet Jesus' sacrifice for mankind was different. It was sufficient. It covered everything. It didn't need an encore or a repeat. It paid for and outdid all the past, present, and future sins of the world. Just as Adam's one sin infected the world, so did Jesus' one sacrifice save those who call upon His name (Heb. 10:14; Rom. 5:12–15).

In summary, mankind cannot attain salvation or right standing before God by anything we do. We must understand we are dead in our trespasses and sins, but God justifies those who believe in the cross's power to pay for our sin and restore us to Himself through our faith in Him (Eph. 2:1–10). We bring nothing to the table except our sin, and in return, God grants us righteousness to Him through faith in Jesus (Rom. 3:21–22). Paul says in 2 Corinthians 5:21 that Jesus became sin on our behalf to face the righteous judgment of God. He came to earth as fully man and fully God, lived a perfectly righteous life, and bore our sins on the cross to pay for the penalty of our sin (Rom. 6:23). How we receive this free gift of salvation is found in Romans 10:9–10: "If you confess with your mouth, 'Jesus is Lord,' and believe in your heart that God raised him from the dead, you will be saved. One believes with the heart, resulting in righteousness, and one confesses with the mouth, resulting in salvation." This, indeed, is good news!

Grace Alone

Saul's conversion is a testament to God's pursuit of His people. Acts 9:4–5 (ESV) tells us, "And falling to the ground, he heard a voice saying to him, 'Saul, Saul, why are you persecuting me? And he said, 'Who are you, Lord?' And he said, 'I am Jesus, whom you are persecuting." In an instant, God appeared to Saul and supernaturally interrupted his life, calling him out of darkness both literally and figuratively. Saul recognized that all the Pharisaical customs, traditions, and attempts at holiness were worthless. He realized his great error against the Son of God and immediate surrender followed. In a matter of seconds, Saul gave up all that he had spent his life building and pursuing to follow Jesus. God used the next three days of Paul's blindness and the next years of journeying to prepare Paul for ministry before connecting with the other apostles. Though God's commission for Paul would be to preach the gospel, even the great apostle's calling was delayed for a season.

The gospel is the message that Saul fought against, but by the grace of God, he surrendered to, and, subsequently, committed himself to preach for the rest of his life. The very man that penned letters in petition to killing Christians penned the hope he once tried to kill off:

> But God proves his own love for us in that while we were still sinners, Christ died for us. How much more then, since we have now been declared righteous by his blood, will we be saved through him from wrath. For if, while we were enemies, we were reconciled to God through the death of his Son, then how much more, having been reconciled, will we be saved by his life. (Rom. 5:8–10)

Paul laid down who he was to step into who God was making him be. His former life was centered entirely around his accomplishments being seen by others. Considering this, it might appear tempting to carry some of those Pharisaical habits into his new relationship with Jesus.

I was a Girl Scout Brownie in first grade. I always felt embarrassed when we would have to wear our vests to school because almost all the other girls in my troop had more patches than I did. If Paul had a Brownie vest, his would be packed with ribbons and medals. However, upon his conversion, this metaphorical vest would be torn off and burnt to ashes. Paul addressed this to the church in Philippi where he describes, "But whatever gain I had, I counted as loss for the sake of Christ" (Phil. 3:7 ESV). As he understood this, so must we understand the worth of knowing Christ is far greater than any earthly accomplishment.

This is the beauty of the gospel: there is no work or physical gift we can offer to God that is worthy of paying the price that Jesus did. This is why when men like Simon the Magician offer money in exchange for the Holy Spirit, Peter rebukes him for thinking God can be bought (Acts 8:9–24). Most of us don't try to purchase salvation with money, but some of us are certainly tempted to think we can work for it in other ways. However, Ephesians 2:9 reminds us that salvation is not by works, eliminating any sort of pride or attempt at bragging about oneself.

Dying to Self

Dying to self is the identifier between an authentic Christian and someone who is just a fan of Jesus. He declares in Luke 9:23–24 (NIV), "Whoever wants to be my disciple must deny themselves and take up their cross daily and follow me. For whoever wants to save their life will lose it, but whoever loses their life for me will save it." Here we see three criteria for the believer who longs to follow Jesus:

1. Self-denial
2. Taking up the cross daily
3. Following or submitting to Him

Jesus stands as the perfect example of a selfless life as He displayed complete dependence on His Father in His earthly ministry, even to the point of death. Throughout the Gospels, Jesus mentions multiple times that He cannot do anything on His own accord and that His desire has never about seeking His own will but rather seeking after His Father's. Another repeated truth is that Jesus never spoke on His own authority but on that of His Father. When He fed empty mouths with physical food, He always pointed back to His Father who offers "true bread from heaven" (John 6:32). Accused and blasphemed for demon possession, Christ attributes His works to His Father to whom He is trying to bring honor. "I do not seek my own glory; there is one who seeks it and judges," Jesus says in John 8:50.

Do you see a pattern here? If the sinless and perfect Jesus could live a life for the honor and glory of the Father, how much more should we who are undeserving of His immeasurable grace live not to ourselves but unto Him? Dying to self simply means putting off or "crucifying" our old ways of selfish, sinful living in recognition of God's ultimate authority in our lives. This is the reality for every Christian as we cannot have new birth in Christ without the death of self. We exchange our will for His will, and our obedience to all He asks of us results in conformity to the image of Christ. We die to self on the day we give our lives to Christ and we continue to die to self as a part of our sanctification process. Though "death to self" sounds scary, it's really just the white flag of surrender to a God who knows better and loves better than we ever could; it's the admission that the chief purpose in our lives is to bring God glory and to follow whatever He asks of us no matter the cost.

The Gospel Changes the Dreamer

I told you we were going to get to the dreaming part. And here we are. Now that we know some of the major parts of the gospel story—this knowledge changes the way the Christian lives (and as a result, how we dream too). When we commit our lives to Christ, we are called to surrender our control over every facet of our living. When I gave my life to God my senior year of high school in the middle of that hotel bathroom, I knew that to truly love God with my whole being, I must lay before Him every piece of my life including the portions I was not willing to give up before.

After repenting of my sin and trusting in Christ for its full payment, I laid before Him all my attempts at self-fulfillment. I asked Him to remove my fleshly desires for love and popularity and give me a heart for Him and His desires alone. For me, this meant I would change my college plans, cut things entirely off with my boyfriend at the time, and seek accountability with my parents. When we commit ourselves to God, we no longer direct our own lives and make plans independent from Him. From the moment of our conversion until our dying breath, we filter every thought, action, and dream through Him and His Word. The fancy word for this is *Lordship*, though really it just means letting God call the shots in your life instead of trusting in yourself to call them. The gospel demands that we lay our desires, our wants, our hopes, our thoughts down and we ask God to be the Lord of our life, for either we are the master of self, or He is the master of us. This decision felt vulnerable and stripped me bare of everything I once held dear. In one sense, it scared me because the future that looked so certain and sure was now at the mercy of the God I had given my life to, but at the same time, it set me free. My future wasn't all on me to muster up. I simply had to follow God's plans, and He was a better navigator of my dreams than I could ever be.

Breaking the Ideal Christian Woman Mold

Though God demands His people be conformed to the image of Christ, He does not desire them to conform to the same cookie-cutter Christian mold we women often force ourselves into. Women's ministry can quickly become a place for this imaginary mold. For many, the ideal Christian woman is married with kids and loves long walks at the parks on playdates. She bakes bread, she sews all her kids' clothing, she serves on several ministry teams at her church, she spends four hours a day reading her Bible, and her house is spotless. She is the definition of a walking, talking Pinterest board whose home, wardrobe, ministry, accomplishments, and crafting abilities are praised by all who view her on social media. She eats strictly organic and non-GMO and would never bring store-bought muffins to a woman's brunch. Her hair is always done, her makeup is perpetually on point, and her and her children's socks always match. She's the Stepford Christian. And though we all know she's not real, we spend our life trying to be her, or angry at all the women who look sort of like her online.

Maybe you are not yet in a season of parenting and feel left out on the playdates, aching for a child. Or maybe parenting conversations make you want to pull your hair out because the moms on the block and in the church don't know how to talk about anything other than their kids. Maybe you are single and you are understandably zoning out on this paragraph right now. Alternatively, perhaps you're a working woman and you miss the women's Bible study altogether because it's clearly designed for women who can be there on a random Tuesday morning when the rest of us are in traffic. There are a thousand areas where we may feel we don't live up to the unspoken standard. When we are so used to looking side to side, it's no wonder we feel lost in these unrealistic expectations.

We are not called to be carbon copies of one another. No, we are called to be like Christ and, therefore, we must fix our gaze upward. Ephesians 2:13–14 says, "But now in Christ Jesus, you who were far away have been brought near by the blood of Christ. For he is our peace, who made both groups one and tore down the dividing wall of hostility." Though Paul wrote this speaking to the division of Gentiles and Jews and proclaiming in Christ they are one, we can apply the truth when it comes to women. Though we are all diverse and different, there should be no division within our ranks—God wants us to be unified. It's the gospel that bridges the gap between the single woman and the married woman and the women with and without kids. It's the gospel that informs every fiber of our being, allowing us to be stuck in traffic on the way home from work while another of us is cooking a casserole (non-organic or organic) to the glory of God. It's the gospel that calls us to lay our preferences down, whether that means engaging in a different worship style or even—can I say it—trying our best at the next women's crafting night that we swore we'd never go to. Though we may end up singing the wrong tune or find ourself featured in a #pinterestfail post, in Christ, we've already detached any value or worth to those skills because He is our supreme worth. He is our identity.

When we grasp this truth, we are free to remove the self-imposed shackles we've placed on ourselves in the name of looking like a model

Christian. It is a beautiful thing when the young and old, the rich and poor, the introvert and extrovert can all gather together in the name of Christ and under the authority of God as different and diverse as we may be, recognizing that no matter how different we are from one another, our calling to Christ remains the same. Dying to self doesn't always mean dying to our personalities, likes, or interests. But it does mean that we all are willing to lay those things down for the sake of one another.

Not All Dreams Die

Death to self doesn't necessarily mean death to our dreams. You may be wondering how this can be when I just spent the entirety of the chapter hashing out how Christians are called to die to self and surrender themselves entirely—dreams included. God knows the desires of our heart. He is very well acquainted with the known and secret things we long for, whether good or bad. The Christian is called to put off those sinful things entirely. We reject what our old nature once desired and pursue the holy living God demands of us. As for desires like the longing for a husband, for kids, for a promotion, or otherwise, the Christian is free to dream of these things so long as she holds these things loosely and entrusts them into God's hands.

We are free to dream, and sometimes God even burdens us with a dream, but these dreams no longer remain first place in our hearts. As new creations in Christ, we now prefer God's will above our own. We pray as Jesus did and say, "Your will be done on earth as it is in heaven" (Matt. 6:10). We are also allowed to dream so long as our dreams do not become our identity. When our self-worth or sense of fulfillment stems from our ambitions, then we can be sure we've misplaced our identity. However, when our identity is firmly rooted in Christ alone, then our dreams become an extension of doing all things for the glory of God, and because we desire His will above our own, we can entrust Him with our dreams and find contentment in whatever it is that He has planned for us.

Our ambitions and passions are not always a bad thing, but we can test what kind of spirit is driving them. The spirit of self-promotion, self-glorification, and building up an earthly kingdom can rear its ugly head inside every one of us, even when our dreams have to do with God or ministry. Instead of a self-obsessed spirit, we should pursue our goals with a spirit of service, humility, and excitement to further God's kingdom purposes, and to His glory.

And if you're struggling to know if your dreams line up with God's will, ask yourself these questions: Does this exalt God or does this exalt self? Am I becoming more like Christ? Can I look back over the past few years and see how God has made me more like His Son? If so, then your dreams are likely becoming more in line with His will.

After all, if you're becoming more like a person, you will naturally dream about the things they do. Here's where I have to check myself often on social media. I'll stumble upon a woman whose sense of fashion or home décor style draws me in. I create mental notes about what it is that I like about her style and an updated shopping list runs in the back of my mind every time I enter Target or the mall. If I'm not careful, my wardrobe or home patterns after her particular taste rather than a mixture of all the eclectic styles I appreciate. I start conforming into her image, and I start dreaming the way she does. The same sort of thing is true of people we actually know in real life. As you grew up, you likely picked up the habits of your close friends—talking how they talked, listening to what they listened to, eating the same sort of foods they ate, and sometimes wanting the same dream job they did. You can't help but become like a person you are constantly around.

This is true with us and the Lord. As we spend time with Jesus, we pick up His habits and His ways of thinking. We start talking like He talks and acting like He acts. The Bible calls this becoming like Him, or conforming to His image. And as we conform more into the image of Christ, so do our dreams conform to God's will.

We start dreaming about the things He desires. We long to see His name promoted, His glory shine, and His kingdom built up. This can happen in a million different ways in a million different industries. For example, have you considered how your dream to, say, grow your business is serving kingdom purposes? Maybe God wants to use it as beacon of light and hope in an industry that glorifies money as the hope worth trusting. Or maybe the clients you are responsible for need to be cared for in a particular way that only a Christian would notice or care about. Perhaps a portion of the proceeds from that business may benefit missionaries raising their support, and in this way, the business plays a part in gospel proclamation. Maybe one of the reasons God has planted the dream of business in you is for the sake of your children—so they can see what godly and balanced work ethic looks like in a workaholic, greedy world. Again—there are a million different ways your dream can serve God's plans. Dying to ourselves doesn't always eliminate our dreams, but it does reshape the way that we dream, how much we value it, and how we handle the outcome of the dream. We can and should still go before God with our ideas and excitements, but our greatest excitement should be for the ways God is working all of it for His own good purposes. Our dreams can be good, but they should not be driving the sole force behind our prayers like it was for me.

Look to the Dream of an Eternity with God

The good news says that Jesus Christ saves us sinners from the curse of the Fall, from ourselves, from death, and from the eternal wrath that was coming for us. He offers justification and forgiveness to those who confess their sin and proclaim Him as Lord of their lives. The gospel bridges any walls of hostility and unites men and women across the world and span of history and time. Despite the different cultural and personal distinctions that may set us apart from one another, the gospel brings unity to diversity. While it calls us to strip ourselves of all preferences and desires for the sake of self, it does not strip us of our individual expression and interests which keep us from conforming to a one-size-fits-all Christian woman mold. The gospel calls us to die to ourselves, and for people like myself and Saul, it may call us to die to our dreams—or what we *thought* was a dream. In other instances, it may not call us to die to our dreams, but it will shape and inform the way we dream.

At the end of our lives, what matters most is not whether or not our dreams come true but whether or not we get to spend an eternity in the presence of God. We will not carry our successes, job titles, and achievements with us to hang on the wall of heaven. Our bank account and Instagram following have zero value when we stand before a Holy God. We can reach the highest heights of success and still fall short of the righteousness needed to stand before the Great Judge. He's not our follower; He's our Lord. He's not impressed with what we deem dream-worthy, shiny as it seems to us, whether that be our influence, our skills, our position, our knowledge, our job, or our résumé. After all, Saul had the most polished résumé of them all and yet was on a path to his own destruction. But God, unimpressed as He was, mercifully intervened out of love, and Paul surrendered all at the foot of the cross when his eyes opened to the truth of the gospel.

Because of the gospel, we have a lasting hope that doesn't fade the way our earthly successes will. We rejoice not in our accomplishments but in Christ's work on the cross which gives us the ultimate prize in life: eternity with our Great God whom we would otherwise be separated from. Jesus remains our example of who it is we are to imitate as we pursue a life of holiness, and faithful men like Paul remind us that God may call us to leave our aspirations behind for better pursuits. As Paul so beautifully describes this in Galatians 2:20 (ESV), "I have been crucified with Christ. It is no longer I who live, but Christ who lives in me. And the life I now live in the flesh I live by faith in the Son of God, who loved me and gave himself for me." The Christian woman, therefore, may lay down her dreams sometimes and pursue them at other times, knowing in each case that her aim is ultimately God's glory and that fulfillment is found in Him alone.

Chapter 4

THE BIGGER STORY

"He made known to us the mystery of his will, according to his good pleasure that he purposed in Christ as a plan for the right time—to bring everything together in Christ, both things in heaven and things on earth in him."

—Ephesians 1:9–10

Imagine living in Europe. Picture, for a moment, sipping an espresso at one of the many charming sidewalk cafes or hiking through one of the old, storybook-like castles. Now consider the possibility of hopping on a train and being in Paris in just a few short hours. This was the new life I had dreamed for us when we heard that the military assigned us to live in Germany. They would pack up all of our belongings, place us in a German apartment or home, and we would spend four years living an inspiring, European lifestyle.

Ethan had a great job but desired to change directions. He filled out paperwork to cross-train in a different field within the military and that meant a new duty station assignment. I had never been to Europe, and Germany was the place I heard Ethan talk so much about. He studied abroad as an exchange student in high school and now speaks the language fluently. I was thrilled at the thought of using my photography skills on a new continent, and Germany became a part of that dream. We were given a few short months to prepare for our new life, and I couldn't wait to see what God had planned for us on that side of the world.

We sold our vehicles, parted with our new puppy to a sweet family (it's difficult and expensive to bring dogs overseas), put our California home on the market, and either sold or passed off many belongings, knowing we had a limited amount of items we could bring overseas. Ethan flew to Georgia to begin his new training while I arranged the last details for our big move. We had everything lined up for Ethan to finish training and for us to ship out to Germany. Our house sold, another confirmation from the Lord (so I thought), and things were looking up. Bring on the espressos and the impromptu outings to Paris.

One week before the movers were to arrive, Ethan called me. "I have bad news," he said in a voice I recognized to be a mixture of sadness and frustration. He informed me that his orders to Germany were canceled. Just like that, someone, somewhere in the great big world that is the military chose to cancel our slot and reassign us to upstate New York. I was absolutely devastated. My mind couldn't wrap around what was happening. The military asked us to base our next four years upon this new dream—a dream which required us to give up so much—and all that we gave up was gone in an instant. Our house was now owned by another—where would we live? All our stuff needed to go somewhere—where would we sleep or sit or eat? Canceled orders meant canceled movers, and I had two weeks to pack up the remnants of our life with a toddler and no husband. And just like that, the boxes that were headed for espressos and jaunts to romantic cities now had nowhere to go. *Why would You put us through this, Lord? You've called us to so many hard things already, and now this too?!*

I felt betrayed. I felt angry. I felt like a child that wasn't getting her way and, in my heart, I threw the biggest adult tantrum. There was absolutely nothing I could do to change the situation and above everything, it's the lack of power over it all that broke me completely.

Once again, I realized I am not in control. But God is. He knew this would happen and this didn't surprise Him. He wrote this into our story, but I didn't like it one bit.

While there are so many worse things that could happen, God used this unmet expectation to fuel my spiritual growth. This cancellation revealed the tight grip I had on moving to Germany. It taught me that, yet again, I had been chasing a dream instead of God. It taught me that though things don't make sense to me, God's thoughts are higher, His ways better. It reminded me that, yes, He is writing my story, but all of this is part of a bigger story.

The Bigger Picture

Each one of us has an ideal script for our lives. We may not have every detail planned out but there are certainly circumstances most would never write in for ourselves. We do not hope for a home foreclosure, cancer diagnosis, or loss of a job. We want the story line where we are in control, our dreams come true, and we live happily ever after. We want espressos and Paris. But the reality is that our lives are filled with unexpected, life-trajectory-changing moments that fragment our lives into little pieces, little boxes that feel like they are going nowhere.

It doesn't take long for us to realize these kinds of experiences aren't only happening to us. One Internet search will reveal this headline (or something like it): "Six Die in a Florida Interstate Crash." What is the reason for this? How do these devastating events and the messy, complex plotlines of our lives fit into God's greater plan? One of the most common phrases spoken in the midst of tragedy is, "Everything happens for a reason." But I always find myself asking: Okay, but what's the reason? And to whom does the world attribute the purpose for these things happening? The Christian would likely say God, and the atheist may attribute nature or the universe. Though each has a different way of interacting with that statement, both the

Christian and the non-Christian cling to it because in moments of trial that are completely out of our control, we desperately desire something or someone to be in control. Religious or nonreligious, we all want to know that it's possible to have a purpose behind pain.

Christ at the Center

Becoming a Christian requires tossing the script we've written for ourselves, trusting in God's plan, and waiting on the Lord to supply the details as they come (if He chooses to let us in on those details). In order to understand our messy life stories, we must first understand God's grand story.

Though I grew up in the church, my experience with Scripture was very fragmented. Long gone are the days of flannel-boards, but I remember them vividly. One of my favorite parts about Sunday school was having the chance to stick one of the felt Bible characters onto the flannel-board as the teacher read a portion from Scripture or summarized that Bible character's life. Simplified versions were easier to digest for the young mind, and so we learned that Noah was obedient because he built a boat, and David was awesome because he slayed a giant. From my perspective these were just a bunch of stories about men and women who were brave and loved God. And yes, they were. But those stories are more than that. The Bible is far from a collection of meaningful, yet disconnected events.

Imagine the Bible as a large tapestry. Up close we find a variety of threads with different textures, colors, and purposes within the tapestry. But if we were to step back far enough with the whole thing in view, we would see one unifying work of art. The overarching purpose and unifying work of Scripture—everything from Genesis to Revelation—is to point to Christ. Consider R. C. Sproul's thoughts on this:

> The Bible is Jesus' story from beginning to end. He is the Alpha and Omega (beginning and the end) of the Bible, even as He is the Alpha and Omega of history. We understand history, we understand the Bible, therefore, only insofar as we understand Jesus. That is what each is for: to show us the glory of the Only Begotten, to the everlasting praise of the Father. May we never, in all our study, lose sight of Him.[1]

If you pay attention, Christ is foreshadowed in the Old Testament and also seen through the New Testament. Let's consider Genesis 22 when God asks Abraham to offer his only son, Isaac, up as a burnt offering on Mount Moriah. At this point in time, he and Isaac (completely unaware of what is about to happen) are making preparations:

> Abraham took the wood for the burnt offering and laid it on his son Isaac. In his hand he took the fire and the knife, and the two of them walked on together. Then Isaac spoke to his father Abraham and said, "My father." And he replied, "Here I am, my son." Isaac said, "The fire and the wood are here, but where is the lamb for the burnt offering?" Abraham answered, "God himself will provide the lamb for the burnt offering, my son." Then the two of them walked on together. When they arrived at the place that God had told him about, Abraham built the altar there and arranged the wood. He bound his son Isaac and placed him on the altar on top of the wood. Then Abraham reached out and took the knife to slaughter his son. (vv. 6–10)

As a child, I found this story to be weird and morbid. I mentally categorized this account into the things-I-will-probably-never-understand file. I didn't learn until my college years this scene foreshadowed Christ.

After Abraham displays his faith and obedience, an angel stopped him and said, "'Do not lay a hand on the boy or do anything to him. For now, I know that you fear God, since you have not withheld your only son from me.' Abraham looked up and saw a ram caught in the thicket by its horns" (vv. 12–13).

In Genesis 12, God made an unconditional covenant with Abraham. A covenant is a promise or agreement between two parties and unlike a conditional covenant which requires both parties to fulfill their ends of the deal, God ensured that this covenant was His alone to fulfill. He promised land, descendants, and redemption to save the world through Abraham's offspring. In the long term, this meant Christ (Gal. 3:16) but in that exact point in time (prior to Christ), that line would have to come through Abraham's physical offspring, Isaac. I bring this up because not only was this Abraham's only child, this was *the* child. This was the one whose lineage would eventually include the Savior, and yet, Abraham trusted God enough to do what He asked. It may also be easy to overlook the fact that Isaac carried wood up the hill (like Jesus carried His cross) to be sacrificed as a burnt offering (or atonement sacrifice). Though Abraham did not have the full view we have, he trusted God when he said, "God himself will provide the lamb for the burnt offering, my son." A ram was provided because the Lamb was yet to come. God would provide His only son, an atonement for our sins, on that very mountain. The words linger—God did not withhold His Son from us. No longer is this a weird, morbid story but rather a beautiful testament to the goodness of God, and a beautiful pointing to Christ. Oh, how we could easily miss that point if we neglect the Word or skim through it quickly.

Right now, I'm teaching my son multiplication. We use flash cards as a resource for memorizing the times tables. He can have all his times tables memorized, but if he doesn't understand the purpose of multiplication in everyday life, it's useless knowledge. The same can be said about our understanding of Scripture. All those years I knew stories about Abraham but my foundation for learning them was built on the wrong concept. "Look at Abraham's obedience! Be like Abraham!" Yes, Abraham had faith and was obedient. Yes, we should live life likewise. But considering we have the full council of God's Word, we can now also say, "Look at Christ's obedience to the point of death on the cross. He is the Lamb who took our place and was slain for our sins. Abraham and Isaac prepared us to see this!" Understanding this changes the way we read Scripture and, as a result, the way we view life and how we can apply certain texts to our outward way of living.

Scripture Is Not Primarily about Me (Or You)

In my early teen years, I collected stacks of teen magazines including but not limited to *Tiger Beat* and *Seventeen* magazine. These were not a helpful source of information for a Christian teenager but the celebrity gossip, makeup tips, and pop band centerfolds kept me coming back for more. I also loved taking the quizzes found inside. It was a tradition for my friends and I to pile our magazine stacks together and work through these. *What kind of a friend are you? Which celebrity are you most like? Is he really into you?* Why is it that these quizzes were so trendy at the time and actually still are? (They just take the form of social media clickbait.) Why is it that tests like the Meyers Briggs or Enneagram have grown increasingly popular? Because we constantly want to learn more about ourselves and be self-aware. We want to know what makes us tick or what it is specifically about our personalities that causes us to function as we do. We assign value to the labels and categories these tests place us in, hoping that by knowing ourselves better we will become better people and live healthier lives.

But Scripture isn't filled with multiple-choice questions with us at the center. It's easier to read that we lack empathy but are great in leadership, as opposed to reading verses that call humanity what it is: sinners desperately in need of a Savior. Whether a *Seventeen* magazine or modern-day personality test, all these calculated Q&As, among many other things, play into the me-centeredness of our culture. And it's this attitude that affects the way we read Scripture.

One common response of the Christian struggling in their Scripture reading is, "I just don't get anything out of it." This is also a me-centered mentality. This response reveals the frustration many of us feel when we open up a text that doesn't appear to relate to where we are in life right now. *What can I get out of this? What is God trying to tell me? How does this make me feel?* In seeking self-diagnosis like that of a personality test, it's our natural tendency to open our Bibles and see where we can find ourselves in the pages. Either one of two things will happen: 1) We read ourselves into every chapter and verse possible, and thereby compromise the intended meaning of the text, or 2) We don't find ourselves immediately and deduce that Scripture is not relevant. If the latter is the case, we usually turn to books that do meet those immediate needs or find our answers elsewhere. When we approach the Bible with "me" as the focal point, we develop tunnel vision and open ourselves to distorting the text—bending and shaping it to meet our needs—or we simply miss out on the riches of certain texts because they do not immediately offer direct application to us.

The problem occurs when we fail to recognize that each portion of Scripture has certain context—it was written during a certain time, to a certain people group, for a certain reason. How confusing it would be for us to open up to Leviticus and try to meditate on the priestly duties for Aaron with ourselves in mind. Yes, all of Scripture applies to us in some way, and there is a point in time when we can seek out application or implications for ourselves, but that is never the first step. Our purpose in reading Scripture is to first learn about God, how He reveals Himself. Consider the original audience, make distinctions between how we differ from that audience, and *then* we can determine how that relates to us. We can't go in with the sole goal of learning about ourselves any more than we open the pages of The Chronicles of Narnia trying to find ourselves on a random page.

There is so much more to glean from the Bible's pages when we consider context. When Jen Wilkin, author of *Women of the Word*, spoke at our *Deeply Rooted Retreat*, she used the illustration of approaching the Bible the way we would approach a letter. When we receive a letter, we don't just tear it open, pick a random paragraph, and claim that as truth for ourselves. No, we examine the letter. Who was it addressed to? Is it even written to me? We check the time stamp. When was it written? And then we open it. What is the purpose of this letter? Typically, we never start in the middle. We start at the beginning and work our way through. We would never open a love letter to someone else and claim its contents for ourselves. This is how we must treat Scripture. We handle it with care and consider the intent of the original author. We should ask questions like: Who was the original audience? (The way a Gentile would read a letter is very different than the way a Jew would.) What cultural gaps do I need to bridge? (Culture in ancient Rome is going to have totally different norms and values than that of Israel.) What genre or literary styles did the author use? (If we turn to the Psalms expecting a narrative, we will be sorely disappointed!) What does this passage teach us about the character of God? The list could go on, but I'd rather you seek out books solely dedicated to studying the Bible if this is a subject you need help with.[2]

From Creation to Consummation

Examining the text with the questions listed above gives us a zoomed-in picture of a certain portion or book of the Bible, but it can also be helpful to zoom out and consider the bigger picture. Scripture is divided into two portions: the Old and New Testaments. This seems like an elementary thing to say, but you'd be surprised how many people don't actually know that. And what are these testaments doing really? What story are they telling? From the beginning of Scripture, sweeping through to the end, there are four major themes or plot points: Creation, the Fall, Redemption, and Restoration. We've explored these four movements in Scripture before, but now we will go into a bit more detail. You'll see that each of these answers a big question that people have always wrestled with throughout human history:

1. Creation (Where did we come from?)

Genesis 1 and 2 cover the span of time when God created life, and everything was as He originally intended. There was perfect peace with God, and God was worshiped as He should be. The time of human history when humans are unaffected by sin is in this portion of Scripture and in parts of Revelation.

2. The Fall (What went wrong?)

We touched a bit on this in chapter 1. Here we find a major plot change when Adam and Eve disobey God's command and listen to the evil advice of the serpent. They rejected God's authority in their lives and their sin separated them from God, resulting in their exile from the garden of Eden. No longer could they walk and talk with the Lord as they once did. Their sin kept them from the presence of a Holy God—they (along with the rest of us) were declared God's enemies. The serpent is cursed, and Adam and Eve enter into a new world, separated by their sin from God, enduring new hardship unlike ever before. The result of the Fall is a world cursed by both spiritual and physical death. Eventually, the law is created as a means of atoning for sin. But as we see throughout the time of Adam and until the time of Jesus, man struggles to keep God's law, repeatedly rejects it, and goes his own way. The need for a Savior remains the ongoing theme.

3. Redemption (What is the answer to our problem?)

But God, being rich in mercy, took the form of man and came down to earth in the most humble way. He lived a perfect life—fulfilling the law in a way no man could. God's masterful plan—spoken of in prophecies long before and awaited by many throughout the Old Testament—finally unfolds. Jesus comes to bring new life to people and free them from the enslavement of sin. He does this by living the life we all should have lived but couldn't, paying for all our sins on the cross, and then—the great climax—conquering the curse of death in the resurrection.

4. Restoration (Where are we going?)

This is the future hope we await. God has given us an inheritance and seat with Him to look forward to. There will one day be a forever with no more pain or tears. Christ will come back a second time to judge the world, and evil will be gone forevermore. A new heaven and earth await those who are in Christ Jesus. Because Jesus conquered death in the resurrection, He set forth a pattern for us—we, too, will resurrect and walk with God again in sinless, immortal bodies and hearts in the renewed creation that is coming. Here, in our resurrected state, we will get to return to our original design of walking with God unhindered by sin or sickness or evil or suffering.

As we consider Scripture from this broader perspective, we learn about the character of God, the consequences of sin and rebellion toward God, the need for the ultimate sacrifice, and the future hope of heaven and eternity with God. As we sort through all these questions in our minds or on paper, we can then ask: How does this passage fit into God's greater story? What does this teach us about God? What does this teach us about man? How does this connect to the gospel? It is in answering these questions that we will understand how to connect our lives to the vertical and horizontal.

At this point you're probably thinking, *I bought this book because I wanted to explore the idea of dream-chasing. I didn't think I was buying a book on Bible study technique.* But here's the thing—the two are irrevocably connected. The fact that we typically think they aren't is the problem! We assume that Scripture is part of our lives in one way—on small group night, during our quiet time, or when we read a Bible story to our kids at night—while our dreams and desires are part of our lives in another way. We compartmentalize the two. But in truth, God wants the way we think, approach, handle, and strategize about our dreams to be steeped in Scripture and in a biblical worldview. In other words, if we are Christians, any and every idea we have (which includes our ambitions and dreams), and any and every plan we make about an idea (which includes our strategies for accomplishing those dreams) should be informed by what God says about Himself, about reality, about the world, and about ourselves. And these things are found in the Bible. We can't talk about our dreams without talking about the Bible. To do so would be like trying make a solid plan for healthy eating or exercise with absolutely no overarching knowledge of how the human body works. And so we must read our Bibles well to do dreaming well.

Reading our Bible is like searching for treasure. Jesus mentions this in Matthew 13:44 (ESV), "The kingdom of heaven is like treasure hidden in a field, which a man found and covered up. Then in his joy he goes and sells all that he has and buys that field." When we look into the Bible, we need to be searching for the treasures God has for us inside His Word and we must be willing to devote our life to it, similar to the man who sold all that he has because he knows how great the treasure is he discovered. Ultimately, we discover that the Bible is one story declaring that there is one God (Exod. 20:3–7; Deut. 4:35; Ps. 86:10), written by one Author (2 Tim. 3:16; 2 Pet. 1:20–21), offering one plan for salvation (John 14:6), and centering around one person—Jesus Christ. It is exciting to make these connections within texts that on a surface level seem so unrelated! It's in these moments that the Holy Spirit illuminates a passage to us that we see He is with us even as we struggle at times through His Word. Considering the themes, knowing the genres, and understanding how all these books tie together is a game changer not only when it comes to reading Scripture, but in walking and living in the truth of Scripture every single day. Context is everything, and knowing and understanding the author's original intent coupled with the grand narrative will greatly enrich your spiritual walk with the Lord and make you a better and more biblical dreamer.

Is Jeremiah 29:11 for the Dreamer?

Jeremiah 29:11 (ESV) is a popular verse that many Christian dreamers claim for their future plans: "For I know the plans I have for you, declares the LORD, plans for welfare and not for evil, to give you a future and a hope." Let's apply some of the things we just learned to this passage. Who is this written to? This portion of Scripture is a historical account with a letter from Jeremiah written specifically to the Israelite exiles. It literally says this in Jeremiah 29:1 (emphasis added): "This is the text of the letter that the prophet Jeremiah sent from Jerusalem *to the remaining exiled elders, the priests, the prophets, and all the people Nebuchadnezzar had deported from Jerusalem to Babylon.*" Then if we skip ahead to verse 4: "This is what the LORD of Armies, the God of Israel, says *to all the exiles I deported from Jerusalem to Babylon.*" There's no second-guessing who this was written to. And while it should be obvious, we should note that we clearly do not fit into the category of exiled Israelites.

What is God's message to these people? God tells the priests, prophets, and people who were recently exiled from their land to make a home in Babylon via planting gardens, building houses, and growing families (vv. 5–6). He encouraged them to pray for the welfare of Babylon as it would directly link to their own welfare (v. 7). And then in verses 8–9 God warns, "Don't let your prophets who are among you and your diviners deceive you, and don't listen to the dreams you elicit from them, for they are prophesying falsely to you in my name.

I have not sent them." He also encouraged them that His plan for their welfare and future still stands despite the fact that they would remain in that land for seventy years (vv. 10–14). Sadly, what we find from verse 15 onward is that the people did not listen to God and the conversation continues when God says:

> "I am about to send sword, famine, and plague against them, and I will make them like rotten figs that are inedible because they are so bad. I will pursue them with sword, famine, and plague. I will make them a horror to all the kingdoms of the earth—a curse and a desolation, an object of scorn and a disgrace among all the nations where I have banished them. I will do this because they have not listened to my words"—this is the LORD's declaration—"the words that I sent to them with my servants the prophets time and time again. And you too have not listened." (vv. 17–19)

Yikes. Do you see the issue here? How can we possibly claim the blessing of 29:11 and yet not claim the curse of 29:17–19? There is valuable context that matters, and if we want to be stewards of all that God has given to us—His Word included—we must carefully consider what it is we are reading. This is not a verse for the dreamer to hang on her wall and imagine that God will give her prosperity in all that she sets her mind to. This is a verse of promise and a word of encouragement to a specific group of people who turned their back on God over and over again and received judgment over and over again, and yet were shown incredible mercy.

The difference between us and them is that we are not exiled Jewish Israelites living in Jeremiah's day. Though this specific promise does not *apply* to us, the general principle we can *imply* from it is this: God loves His people and will not abandon them. Though He passed judgment, He is faithful to His covenants. As New Testament

Christians, we can look at this and praise Him for His patience and mercy, and cling to our own unshakable security in Jesus knowing that, despite whatever hardship we face in this lifetime, our future hope awaits us in the coming resurrection and new heavens and earth. However, the dreamer cannot attach this verse to her dreams if she values the integrity of Scripture. She cannot paste Jeremiah 29:11 on her plans to, for example, open a business, assuming God is now on the hook to make all her career dreams come true. Her business is not the "hope and future" God was talking about in Jeremiah. While the eternal "hope and future" for all believers is the same (heaven), God's temporary plan for the exiled Israelites in Babylon here in Jeremiah 29:11 is not the same temporary plan God may have for you and I here in the twenty-first century. We can trust that God certainly has a plan for our lives both eternally and in the here and now, but we cannot assume His plan guarantees worldly success in every season.

Clear Perspective

After an evening of writing at a nearby coffee shop close to the city, I drove back to our home in the country. We are surrounded by farmland with hardly any lights around. On a clear sky, thousands of stars show themselves off in the most intricate fashion. As I stepped out of my car that winter night, I looked up in wonder at the personal planetarium in my own backyard. For a moment I felt removed from everything and stood there simply in awe, praising God. My thoughts were not occupied with my writing deadline. I wasn't wondering if my husband had successfully put our kids to sleep. I didn't even notice that it was twenty-something degrees outside. The skyline before me was magnificent, and in those moments my immediate world became very small.

How great a chasm there was between me and these balls of fire. And what of their vantage point of me? I was a speck—no, I was less than a speck on this huge earth. I began to think about all the other specks like me living their lives completely unaware of the vastness of our great universe, and the One whose presence extends far beyond those cosmic borders. But this moment wasn't unique to me. Many songs have been written about the beauty of the stars or the sharing of the same night sky, but they are written in the context of here and now—one moment in time. As I considered each life centuries before me and those who may stand in awe centuries from now, my time line in the history of the world grew even smaller. This, I imagine, is how the psalmist felt when he penned: "When I observe your heavens, the work of your fingers, the moon and the stars, which you set in place, what is a human being that you remember him . . . ?" (Ps. 8:3–4). The very God who created and sustains this breathtaking universe is the same God who created you and me. He fashioned us in His image and knows us intimately. He is a God that tells us He is working all things for good for those who are called according to His purpose (Rom. 8:28). Therefore, we can trust that He is orchestrating all the details in our own personal "speck" within the big picture.

Recently, a mentor shared a story from a funeral that she attended. The pastor talked about how life is a "vapor that appears for a little while, then vanishes" (James 4:14). If you've been a Christian for any period of time, I'm sure you have heard this verse. But what surprised her was when he held up a small bottle, and with the push of a finger he sprayed some sort of liquid. There in a place where the life of someone was there one day and gone the next, funeral attendees saw an actual mist that was there for a second and gone the next. This visual demonstrated the very thing we've read and heard said over and over. It impacted her greatly, as hearing about it did me.

God graciously provides us with these sorts of visuals—from vapors to the stars—to give our human minds some sort of comprehension of His vantage point. It is so easy to get fixed on our present circumstances, our pain, and even our ambitions and dreams, and live our lives as if what is before us is all there is. But the Christian knows better. We need not be so busy navel-gazing that we forget to look up at the stars and consider Who made them. This is why we should read through Scripture paying close attention to the grand narrative. It helps us remember the specks we are—and that our dreams are—in the bigger story. This doesn't mean that we don't matter to God or that our dreams are insignificant to Him. It simply frees them from looking like the biggest deal in the world to us. It relieves the pressure. It puts things in proper proportion. It helps us see things the way they actually are. We will profit much as we consider our day-to-day moments in light of eternal realities. The truth of Scripture and the future hope for the Christian changes absolutely everything for us, including our passions, dreams, and pursuits. Though God is not bound by time, we are placed on a real time line. Like the Israelites who awaited their Messiah, we await His second coming, and while we wait, we must be faithful to what He has called us to presently.

A Dream Laid Down

Just as quickly as Germany was canceled, so was our assignment to New York. Ethan injured himself, which delayed him from continuing his training, and the decision he faced was whether he would stay there, recover, and continue training, or if he would just withdraw from this new job altogether and go back to his original position. After weeks of sitting in a hotel room waiting to be seen by a doctor, he felt a peace about withdrawing his cross-training paperwork and returned home. However, the problem remained: we had already sold our home, and now Kaiden and I were homeless. Ethan wouldn't be discharged for several weeks to come. Since there was no new assignment for us, the movers that the military would have paid for to Germany or New York were canceled and it was entirely up to me to figure out where we would live and what we do with all our stuff in the meantime. The base housing list was full, and I could not find any rentals available that we could afford.

We couldn't even afford moving boxes, so I drove around from grocery store to grocery store looking for any extras. "I'm not supposed to give you these," the chips delivery man said, but he handed me some anyway. *Thank You, Lord.* And then I discovered someone offering free moving boxes on Craigslist. *Thank You, Lord.* And then, someone tipped me off that beverage stores have the best boxes because they can carry such heavy weight. So, I went by their trash area behind the store and hit the jackpot. *Thank You, Lord.* I couldn't believe how elated I was to have such a collection of boxes, but in those moments I saw clear provision. God had called us to this difficult circumstance, but He would lead us through it.

My mom flew out to help us, and alongside a few men from our church and Ethan's work, we moved the most essential remnants of our life and placed it all into a 12x30 storage unit. I didn't know if Ethan needed surgery or when he would even come home. I didn't know where our next assignment would be or where we would even live a month from that point in time, but I knew the truth about God. He is our Provider. If He cares about the birds, then He cares about me (Matt. 6:26–27; Job 38:41). This was not a mistake or an oversight on His part. No, these messy, confusing details of my life somehow fit into His grand plan. Also, we were not alone in our struggles. The Bible offers many examples of painful, confusing moments that all add up to one, beautiful truth. He is in control, writing a bigger story, and I can rest in that.

Kaiden and I lived at my best friend's house on base for a little over a month. In God's perfect timing, Ethan came home—more broken than when he left but not in need of surgery—and just like that, a house on base that was meant for a larger family opened up and was given to us, despite the long waiting list. The details were already predetermined and unfolding before us, we just had to trust in God.

In one moment, we went from moving to our dream country, Germany, to temporary homelessness, but I believe the Lord used that situation to change my heart, teach us to trust Him, show off

His generous provision, and reveal to me that He is enough. The work He did in my heart over those months was far more valuable to my soul than any tangible European dream I could have hoped for. Every location He has moved us to, every new neighbor we meet, and every hardship that comes with the territory all points back to God's sovereign hand. He desires to work through us where we are—for our good and His glory.

In the end, though God certainly cares about our ambitions, passions, and dreams, He cares more about our obedience and our submission to Him, our holiness through sanctification—which is making us more like Christ. That's what He was doing in me during that season of confusion and loss (by the world's standards)—making me a person that wanted God more than I wanted some European dream to come true. He was making me into a person who didn't need the dream in order to be happy in Him. And that was worth every moment of the experience.

While many times the common phrases of our culture can get it wrong, there's one that is right: There *is* a reason for everything. And Christians know what that reason is. We know that God has written one grand story and we can remain confident and hopeful because we already know the end. Whether an Israel-exile or dreamer in the twenty-first century, we rest not in our present circumstances but in what is yet to come. When we harden our hearts during these difficult and stressful times, we fail to see our lives in relation to God's faithful character. We also blind our eyes from seeing God at work. He uses our weakness as a means of displaying His great power and proving that His grace is sufficient, just as He has many men and women of the past. This is not to belittle the painful hardships so many are currently walking through. Scripture affirms the realities of hardship in a believer's life. By keeping the grand narrative in mind, though, we are able to step back like specks before stars and rest in His perfect plan. In stepping back, we remember God. When the weight of present realities bears heavy on our hearts, we have this assurance from 1 Peter 1:3–9:

> Blessed be the God and Father of our Lord Jesus Christ. Because of his great mercy he has given us new birth into a living hope through the resurrection of Jesus Christ from the dead and into an inheritance that is imperishable, undefiled, and unfading, kept in heaven for you. You are being guarded by God's power through faith for a salvation that is ready to be revealed in the last time. You rejoice in this, even though now for a short time, if necessary, you suffer grief in various trials so that the proven character of your faith—more valuable than gold which, though perishable, is refined by fire—may result in praise, glory, and honor at the revelation of Jesus Christ. Though you have not seen him, you love him; though not seeing him now, you believe in him, and you rejoice with inexpressible and glorious joy, because you are receiving the goal of your faith, the salvation of your souls.

Our end goal is not the here and now; it is the salvation of our souls and the future we have with Jesus in the resurrection. He has given us new birth, a living hope, an inheritance that is imperishable, undefiled, and unfading! We are guarded by God's power for a salvation to be revealed in the last days. We can rejoice in trials not just to prove our faith but refine us, sanctify us, and grow us in holiness. The grand narrative helps us to view our life in light of the bigger picture and the promises for the Christian life help us to understand how intimate and personal our God is for every believer no matter where in history (or His story) you fit into. We who deserve nothing and yet have been given everything.

When our dreams don't fall into place as we had hoped, when everyone around us appears to be more successful, when our Germany assignment falls through, we can look upward and trust that God is working these things together for our good. His ultimate aim for our lives is holiness and He uses these "light and momentary troubles" (2 Cor. 4:17 NIV) and adversities to fulfill that end. Ephesians 1:4–5 (ESV) says: "Even as he chose us in him before the foundation of the world, that we should be holy and blameless before him. In love he predestined us for adoption to himself as sons through Jesus Christ, according to the purpose of his will . . ." The God who created us chose us long before He even created the world. He already determined ahead of time that we would be holy and blameless. Turn to Scripture with the knowledge that God has always worked in beautiful and mysterious ways to redeem a people for Himself. As you consider the context, themes, and genres you will learn so much more about God, and thereby understand yourself within this story. Both the big picture and the small details within the whole point back to God and His glorious purposes.

The good news in all of this is that God has something better than a dream for me and you, and for all His people—He has a divine *will* for us all, and it always comes true. God's will for His people and the bigger story that we each are a part of—*will* come true. Most of it already has, actually. And while our specific dreams in specific seasons aren't always guaranteed, His will is. Hear this and rest in it: If you've committed your life to Him, God's will for you is *going* to come true. You are *going* to be conformed into the image of Christ. You are *going* to be fully resurrected and glorious one day, and you are *going* to live with Christ forever in a sinless and restored world. There's no greater dream than that, and you are guaranteed it.

Chapter 5

THE FRUITFUL DREAMER

"My Father is glorified by this: that you produce much fruit and prove to be my disciples."

—John 15:8

It's easy to grow bitter when your entire life revolves around your husband's job. This is especially true for military families. A military member's job dictates every aspect of their lives including but not limited to where they will move, when they can vacation, and even how often they see their own family.

Ethan was in and out of our home for various training assignments and deployments, and it affected my son in ways I did not anticipate. I would catch Kaiden roaming the upstairs looking for his dad. Any time he heard a truck pull into our neighborhood, our dog would bark, and Kaiden would race to the door with the expectation that his dad was home. There were always tears to wipe. The inconsistency of a parent jumping in and out of the life of a child creates instability in that child's world, and it is hard on a wife and mom to play her own roles, plus her husband's.

Without a job in photography, the only visible "purpose" in my life that I could see was supporting my husband in his career and helping my baby grow into a child. I had the head knowledge that there is immense value in these things, but how do you really encapsulate all of that when you're at a social function and are asked, "What do you do for a living?" I never did know how to respond to that question. It wasn't long before I learned to hide in the shadow of my husband's career. "I'm a stay-at-home mom and military wife, but my husband is a survival specialist."

The technical term is a SERE Specialist. SERE is an acronym for survival, evasion, resistance, and escape in the military. I was and still am very proud of his accomplishments and achievements. It's so easy for me to rattle off story after story, like his surprise graduation test where he was dropped off in the middle of nowhere in a snowy winter with nothing but a dull knife, a rabbit, and a thin jumpsuit to survive for an unknown number of days. Or the time when he deployed to Iraq and was a part of a rescue for many Christian Yazidis who were cut off and surrounded by ISIS forces. As far as I could see, my life only amounted to struggles with diapers, dishes, and the endless answering of toddler questions. Buried deep below my struggles of discontent and purposelessness was gratitude, but more often than not it suffocated underneath all the negative feelings. While Ethan attended jungle training courses in the Philippines, I was trying to tame the jungle-like mess my toddler made. While he was jumping out of planes, I was lecturing Kaiden to not jump on the couch. I was happy that Ethan had many opportunities to maintain his qualifications and sharpen his skills, but I struggled to find contentment in the mundane tasks of my day-to-day while Ethan's life looked so extraordinary.

We had many conversations about the fact that although his job was fun, it was still a job and wasn't always 100-percent recreation. It paid the bills, provided incredible health care, and he had many stressors and dangers that I didn't face. I listened to him as he confessed his envy that I had the opportunity to spend whole days with our son while he only had a few hours with Kaiden until bedtime. He wished he could have the schedule I had, and he longed for the freedom from regimented military rules. As I look back now, I see that we both thought the grass was greener in one another's fields, and I'm so grateful to God that Ethan remained a patient listener and encourager as I worked through all my emotions.

While I was still in the thick of the struggle, I didn't just compare myself to my own husband. I compared myself to many of the strangers I followed on social media. Their feeds displayed lives of contentment, peace, and joy. Each refresh of my feed notified me about someone's new house remodel or another's summer-long vacation. Here were wives who had their husband's home on a regular basis or moms who lived near family and had help with their kids. Each highlight of one individual's life snowballed into one massive conglomeration of lives I wasn't living.

While I didn't actively grumble or complain all the time, it didn't take much for the grumbles and complaints to leave my lips. I tried to make the most out of the time we had when Ethan was home, but it was my reactions to situations that revealed what was buried deep within my heart: seeds of discontent, restlessness, and envy. For example, if Ethan would ask me to change a dirty diaper after a few weeks of being away, a running tally in my mind of how many dirty diapers I've had to change would spur me toward an angry reaction. There was a war waging within. There were days where I felt completely content in the life God had called me to, but there were other days where I was just worn out from it all. These negative emotions I felt stood in stark contrast with the call to holy living I knew I had committed my life to. I tried my best to take my thoughts and emotions captive but in my own strength, it was a losing battle.

A Tree Is Known by Its Fruit

"If you plant an apple tree, you will get?" "Apples!"
"If you plan an orange tree, you will get?" "Oranges!"
"If you plant a lemon tree, you will get?" "Avocadoes!"

We chose to homeschool our kids for a year and every now and then, one smarty-pants would purposefully throw in a wrong answer just to be silly. I asked this series of questions to illustrate to my kids that the fruit produced by a tree correlates with the tree itself. Of course, an apple tree will produce apples. We know this because a tree is known by its fruit. I attempted to explain what the fruit of the Spirit looks like in the Christian's life based on Galatians 5:22, emphasizing that love, joy, peace, patience, kindness, goodness, faithfulness, gentleness, and self-control are produced from the Holy Spirit—they are not traits we can muster up in our own strength. When we abide in Him, we produce the fruit He gives. A Christian is known by her fruit.

The question is: Do I bear fruit? As I look back at my life with photography or in the early stages of motherhood and military life, I see a lot of what Scripture calls "works of the flesh" (Gal. 5:19). I allowed my circumstances and my emotions to dictate my moods, outlook on life, and my actions. Scripture says:

> Hard times will come in the last days. For people will be lovers of self, lovers of money, boastful, proud, demeaning, disobedient to parents, ungrateful, unholy, unloving, irreconcilable, slanderers, without self-control, brutal, without love for what is good, traitors, reckless, conceited, lovers of pleasure rather than lovers of God, holding to the form of godliness but denying its power. (2 Tim. 3:1–5)

We live in a culture where these vices are not only common but accepted and sometimes even praised. Worldly thinking is a result of fleshly living, but guess what? It isn't just found in the external places like motivational quotes, movies, and magazines like we talked about in chapter 1. It is found within. Within you and within me. Daily there is an ongoing battle between our flesh and spirit waging war within us. We do the things we shouldn't do, and we don't do the things we should. We cry out in frustration with Paul: "What a wretched man I am! Who will rescue me from this body of death?" (Rom. 7:24). The problem of sin within us is real because we battle two natures: the old nature that was passed to us from Adam and the new nature given to us by the Spirit. Our old nature rises up within and manifests itself within us in different ways as it did within my attitude toward my husband and home. Galatians 5:19–21 provides a list of these fleshly habits:

> Now the works of the flesh are obvious: sexual immorality, moral impurity, promiscuity, idolatry, sorcery, hatreds, strife, jealousy, outbursts of anger, selfish ambitions, dissensions, factions, envy, drunkenness, carousing, and anything similar. I am warning you about these things—as I warned you before—that those who practice such things will not inherit the kingdom of God.

We know, however, that this list is not exhaustive since Paul tacks on "and anything similar" to the end of the lengthy list. This means that the comparison and discontent I wrestled with also fit into works of the flesh. These areas of living are opposite to how the Christian should conduct herself. Once again, we find that God takes sin seriously for Paul warns that those who practice these very things "will not inherit the kingdom of God." Sin is what kicked Adam and Eve out of the garden and it's what keeps those who practice these things eternally separated from God. The people who make an ongoing practice of these things provide clear and obvious indication that they are not children of God.

In contrast to these "works" of the flesh, Galatians 5 continues with the "fruit" of the Spirit:

> But the fruit of the Spirit is love, joy, peace, patience, kindness, goodness, faithfulness, gentleness, and self-control. The law is not against such things. Now

> those who belong to Christ Jesus have crucified the flesh with its passions and desires. If we live by the Spirit, let us also keep in step with the Spirit. Let us not become conceited, provoking one another, envying one another. (vv. 22–26)

These verses provide clear indicators of what a Christian looks like. As opposed to hatred, the Christian bears the fruit of love. The Christian isn't anxious but is at peace. She isn't cruel, but kind. There isn't badness, disloyalty, or harshness but rather there is goodness, faithfulness, and gentleness. Our fruit-bearing ability is not dependent on pleasant circumstances, as it shows forth even amidst the toughest of calamities. All in all, the Holy Spirit should characterize the way we think, act, and, thereby, live. The problem with this—the reason we have such a hard time embodying this fruit day-to-day—is the inner battle I mentioned earlier of our old nature versus new nature. Becoming spiritually mature and bearing much fruit doesn't happen instantly and effortlessly. It requires human cooperation. This is how works of the flesh may easily take root in our lives if we allow them to. This means that the Christian will make mistakes sometimes. But ultimately, he or she should not have a consistent pattern of sin in their lives. And that includes the patterns of sin that come particularly with dream-chasing.

The Struggles for the Dreamer Are Real

Comparison

Want to know the perfect recipe for comparison? Take a cup of envy, add in another cup of covetousness, and throw in a heaping pile of social media. Our six-inch screens give us a front-row seat to the world's #bestlifenow. But comparison is a deadly trap. It takes our eyes off of the blessings before us and fixes them on everyone around us.

Rather than clinging to the truth of Scripture and fixing our eyes on great, heavenly realities, these palm-sized snippets into other people's lives become our standard for living and our measure for self-worth. Comparison manifests itself in one of two ways: either we develop a spirit of pride or of insecurity. Pride tells us we are better than others and insecurity tells us we are not enough. Regardless of which way we compare, looking side to side skews our view and creates an insatiable desire for whatever definition of success we have created in our minds. We then exhaust ourselves working to either attain it or maintain it.

Remember the Christian photographer mentor and friend that introduced me to Ikea, Thai food, and bubble tea? It was not long into our friendship that I began to compare my life to hers. Every inquiry she received was an inquiry I didn't receive. Her success revealed my insecurities and lack of success. But basic science acknowledges that a slight change of variables will result in a different outcome. For example, the state of water responds to different temperatures. My problem is that I was expecting the same results of success as my friend when we had different life variables. Never mind the fact that she had a network of family and friends in the area we had just moved to. Never mind that she was established several years before me. Never mind that she was simply more talented than I was. God determined two different paths for our lives in a thousand other ways, but I was so fixated on having the same story in this one particular area. We do ourselves, others, and our dream a disservice when we compare and expect a similar outcome. Comparison does nothing to benefit ourselves or the one we are comparing ourselves to.

Discontent

Sin doesn't live in isolation. Where one finds comparison there is likely discontent. Greed overtakes our heart and makes demands that we deserve whatever God has chosen to give the person whose circumstances we covet. Not only do we miss out on rejoicing over what God has already given us, we miss the opportunity to rejoice with others over the opportunities God has given them. Discontent creates a spirit of unrest, and we remain dissatisfied until we receive what we demand. The problem is when we do receive it, that satisfaction is temporary. Feeding our discontent only fuels more discontent. Rather than declaring, "The Lord is my portion" (Lam. 3:24), we declare that what the Lord has willed for us presently is not enough.

Selfish Ambition

Another sin that likes to hang around these two is selfish ambition. The world as it is now is set up to spotlight me, myself, and I. With websites named YouTube and platforms that instantly connect us with people across the world, there are endless ways to self-promote. Opposite of making God's fame known throughout the world, selfish ambition likes to make our fame known. Philippians 2:3–4 discourages this mind-set: "Do nothing out of selfish ambition or conceit, but in humility consider others as more important than yourselves. Everyone should look out not only for his own interests, but also for the interests of others." Selfish ambition is focused on our own personal glory, and when we are wholly focused on promoting our own interests and agendas, we forget that we are here for the glory of God and His mission to go and make disciples. We also miss out on caring for the interests of others. This verse makes it clear that there is necessity in looking out for our own interests to a degree, but we do so with open eyes aware of the needs of those around us to that very same degree, if not a higher one.

These are just a few works of the flesh common to dreaming, and Christians are not immune to these tendencies. Consider this illustration: Imagine that I bought a vehicle that requires premium gasoline, or maybe even diesel, but instead I fill it with regular, unleaded gas. This neglect will not change the outward appearance of the car, but it will destroy the inside. The car may run for a short season but there will be signs and symptoms that signal its destruction. In the same way, when the Christian who is meant to be filled by the Spirit fills herself with nothing but the concerns of the flesh, her fate is surely inward decay. Her selfish ambition, discontent, and comparison may drive her to live a beautiful life that attracts a large following and gives the appearance that she is totally fine outwardly, but inwardly, if she is truly in Christ, she will be miserable. Worse than that, she will be compromised spiritually before the Lord Himself.

It's easy to point our finger at the areas where we most obviously notice bad fruit manifesting itself in our lives, but it's harder yet to solve the bad fruit. Many times, we simply try to cut out our bad behavior or change the circumstances that are "causing" us to act in fleshly, unfruitful ways. We assume the circumstances are the problem. *If we just weren't struggling financially, I wouldn't act this way. If that coworker would just act right, I wouldn't respond the way I did at our meeting yesterday. If my kids just listened to me the first time, anger wouldn't rear its ugly head the way it did just now.* But the circumstances aren't the problem. We are. The circumstances just offer the stage in which the hidden sin comes out and presents itself to the world. For me the sins I struggled with weren't simply because of my husband's schedule or my attempts at chasing after my dreams—whether that be photography or Germany or otherwise. A change of schedule for my husband or a "new life purpose" to call my own may have put a Band-Aid on the issue, but it would not remove the deeper ailment within. No, the "works of the flesh" had manifested themselves in my life because I was not "walking by the Spirit" as Scripture commands me to (Gal. 5:16). The fruit coming out of my life simply showed where my roots were getting nourished—flesh instead of Spirit.

The Holy Spirit: Power for Holy Living

Last year we spent a weekend with some of our good friends and their families in the Poconos. We shared a two-story cabin that was spacious, cozy, and the perfect size for adults to hang out and little ones to roam around. At one point I ran upstairs to grab something from our room and, as I hurried back downstairs, I slipped and fell. Somehow, I missed the last two steps and the result was a painful blow to the knee. One would think I would be a little more cautious but later that day, in my clumsiness, I missed the last steps again and fell once more. My husband likes to call me "crazy legs" and "crazy arms" because I have a tendency toward klutziness, but I didn't understand why it was a clear struggle for me to get down those stairs. It was not until we arrived home and I went down our own staircase that I understood what happened. We have thirteen stairs, which means by "step" number fourteen, my feet are planted firmly on the ground. The cabin had around sixteen stairs, a platform, and then another set of three or four stairs. Apparently, I had a bad case of muscle memory. Moving down our thirteen stairs was a habit and, embarrassingly enough, a hard habit to break.

Similarly, when we are used to operating in our flesh, it's natural for our everyday reactions to recall "muscle memory." When we've lived in a spirit of comparison, discontent, lust, and anger for so long it becomes an engrained reaction to much of life. We're used to the same old steps, and to walk a different way, we must intentionally re-train ourselves in the power of the Holy Spirit to discard our former way of living and embrace the new life—and responses to life—Jesus calls us to. First Peter 2:1 says "rid yourselves of all malice, all deceit, hypocrisy, envy, and all slander." Ephesians 4:22 says to "take off your former way of life, the old self that is corrupted by deceitful desires." If those lists look daunting to you, it's because you can't do them without God. But by the power of the Holy Spirit, we *can* react in a spirit of patience as opposed to anger. We *can* respond in words of love and humility rather than pride. And here's the assurance found in Galatians 5:16: "I say then, walk by the Spirit and you will certainly not carry out the desire of the flesh." Did you catch the beautiful promise? "Walk by the Spirit and you will *certainly not* carry out the desire of the flesh" (emphasis mine). As Christians, we have this guarantee. In the Holy Spirit, *yes we can* live and respond like Jesus does.

In other words, we are no longer slaves to sin, we are now slaves to Christ. We see this truth all throughout Scripture:

- "Therefore, if anyone is in Christ, he is a new creation; the old has passed away, and see, the new has come!" (2 Cor. 5:17).
- "I have been crucified with Christ, and I no longer live, but Christ lives in me. The life I now live in the body, I live by faith in the Son of God, who loved me and gave himself for me" (Gal. 2:20).
- "Don't you know that if you offer yourselves to someone as obedient slaves, you are slaves of that one you obey—either of sin leading to death or of obedience leading to righteousness?" (Rom. 6:16).
- "But now, since you have been set free from sin and have become enslaved to God, you have your fruit, which results in sanctification—and the outcome is eternal life!" (Rom. 6:22).

Both the Christian and the non-Christian may wrestle with works of the flesh, but only one has the ability to be freed from their grips. The Christian is freed from the bondage of sin in her life! These verses plainly state that we are no longer trapped or enslaved to our former ways. *We really don't have to respond to life the way we used to. We really aren't bound by those old tendencies.* Rather than practicing a life that leads to death, we have been given eternal life and the power to live a holy life right here, right now. To turn back to our old habits and works of the flesh is to neglect our greatest Source for Christian living: the Holy Spirit.

It's the difference between trying to serve God in our own strength versus the power He readily gives us in the Spirit. Imagine you are a well-crafted lamp in a dark room. Apart from being connected to a power source (an outlet), your lamp has no ability to shine light on its own. Yet we go through life this way, trying to live out our calling and let our lights shine (via the bearing of fruit) without being connected to the power source. It's entirely impossible!

If we live by the Spirit, we will bear the very fruit we long for. Love is not found in a boyfriend or marriage. Peace is not found in self-care or yoga. Joy is not found in attaining every earthly comfort. All these things and more are found in God alone! We must quit living as though the success of our dream, or the accumulating of material goods, or whatever it may be for us, is going to satisfy us.

So how do we do this? Rather than the Lord providing a list of rules we are to follow, He gives us His Spirit to be dependent upon. We must recognize that fruitful living is yet another thing we are dependent on God for. The fruitful woman preaches to herself, "I am able to do all things through him who strengthens me" (Phil. 4:13). If you are weary and exhausted from attempting to piece together some semblance of peace in your home, rest in God's strength. If you are worn from the restlessness of discontent and worldly passions waging war within you, again I say, rest in God's strength. If God is calling you to lay down a dream, or perhaps pursue one for His glory, both of these things require God's strength to accomplish! We cannot surrender or lay down a dream without the Lord's help, without His strength helping pry our fingers open from the death grip we've had on a dream we thought would make everything better in our lives. And on the flip side, we also have no hope of pursuing a dream He is calling us to act upon without His strong hands doing the heavy lifting. The call to Christian living, including what we do with our dreams, cannot be lived independent of the power of God. Otherwise, we exhaust ourselves in our self-sufficient striving and we become frustrated when we fall short of any fruit-bearing standards we've set for ourselves. If you're anything like me, you don't wake up in the morning wanting to be consumed with the works of the flesh when it comes to dream-chasing in particular—comparison, envy, discontent, and so on. You really do want to embody the fruit of the Spirit instead. You just need to know how. And Jesus tells you (and me). In John 15:1–8, Jesus illustrates the very model for fruitful, Christian living:

> "I am the true vine, and my Father is the gardener. Every branch in me that does not produce fruit he removes, and he prunes every branch that produces fruit so that it will produce more fruit. You are already clean because of the word I have spoken to you. Remain in me, and I in you. Just as a branch is unable to produce fruit by itself unless it remains on the vine, neither can you unless you remain in me. I am the vine; you are the branches. The one who remains in me and I in him produces much fruit, because you can do nothing without me. If anyone does not remain in me, he is thrown aside like a branch and he withers. They gather them, throw them into the fire, and they are burned. If you remain in me and my words remain in you, ask whatever you want and it will be done for you. My Father is glorified by this: that you produce much fruit and prove to be my disciples."

This is how we bear fruit: by abiding in Jesus. Fruit cannot happen apart from the Vine, and Jesus is our Vine. He's our power source. Notice the direct tie-in to our Galatians verses about the person who practices the works of the flesh and doesn't inherit the kingdom of God (5:19–21). This exact person who doesn't bear fruit is removed, thrown aside, withered, and burnt up. But the one who proves to be His disciple produces much fruit—something she cannot muster up apart from Jesus.

Tools for Fruitful Christian Living

So, as we've seen, fruitful living simply means abiding in Christ. He has not only given us the command to abide in Christ and therefore bear fruit, but He's also given us the ways to obey that command. He tells us to stay connected to the Vine, to tap into the Holy Spirit's strength, and to bear much fruit. And then He gives us all the tools we need to do those very things. Mind you, this is not meant to be a legalistic list to encourage upright living for the sake of upright living. Instead, we engage these things as a response to all God has done for us in Christ. We do these things because they simply help connect us to the Vine, and as we do, we are inwardly transformed by the power of the Holy Spirit who affects our outward way of living.

1. Bible Reading

Have you ever noticed that people lean toward being more of a drink person or a food person? My mother-in-law is a great example of someone who remains hydrated. She's always sipping on something. Her sweet pleasure is Diet Coke, and on a warm day, you might also see her with sweet tea. But her primary drink is water—cup filled to the brim with ice cubes and all. I, on the other hand, eat way more than I drink. I love appetizers, snacks, and food in general. Whenever I go out to a restaurant with her, the waitress has probably circled our table four or five times to refill her water, each time signaling a reminder that I should probably take another sip of that water that's not even an inch down from the cup line. The result of my consistent forgetfulness and carelessness is fatigue and dizzy spells throughout the day. Whenever I complain, my husband chimes in, "How much water have you had to drink today?" I don't know why I am in the habit of not drinking water—something essential to well-being and very life.

Bible reading is like water that nourishes our souls. It gives us vitality. I'm sure I sound like a broken record but I cannot emphasize enough how important it is to our abiding in Jesus. It is essential to our Christian living because it gives us the ability to commune with God. When we neglect the Word, we become spiritually parched and malnourished. And similar to my experience with actual water, symptoms inevitably show up when we fail to "drink our water" for the day. We get foggy, tired, and out of sorts, spiritually speaking. Our souls become lethargic and sluggish and irritable. We know there's a well of water sitting right there, waiting for us to drink as much as we need, but we siphon off a teaspoon every now and then wonder why we feel spiritually disoriented, discontent, or distant. And because we won't hydrate on what will keep us healthy, we shrivel up spiritually, like raisins on a vine in the place where a grape should be.

We know that "All Scripture is inspired by God and is profitable for teaching, for rebuking, for correcting, for training in righteousness, so that the man of God may be complete, equipped for every good work" (2 Tim. 3:16–17). This passage helps us realize that the Bible is not a mere guidebook for holy living or a check in the box to affirm our Christian duty. It is not an instruction manual that sits on our bookshelf as a resource "just in case" we need it. Instead, it is the way God chooses to reveal Himself to us and it offers us the "training in righteousness" we need so that we can be fruitful and perform good works! On top of this, the Bible is "living and effective . . . sharper than any double-edged sword" (Heb. 4:12). It cuts straight to our core as we engage with it, helping us to evaluate our hearts. It reads us as we read it.

The dreamer who remains rooted in the Word understands that a neglect of the Word is essentially a neglect of God. She does not want to be tossed back and forth between her dreams and what she thinks may be God's will. She knows she cannot know His will for herself if she doesn't know Him, how He works, and what He desires of His people. This dreamer knows the Bible gives us an account of all of those things. It sets the standard for what God calls good, holy, and honoring to Him. She gleans much as she observes those who have angered God and those who have pleased Him. She recognizes that Bible reading is essential to her dreaming because it provides a standard to compare her dreams to.

2. Prayer

Chasing dreams often results in long to-do lists and never-ending seasons of busyness. Prayer, however, puts a halt to all of that. It is an intentional slowing down to be still before the Lord and acknowledge our utter dependence on Him. Let's face it: it's easier to "put feet to our prayers" and focus on making things happen on our own time and in our own strength. We may see immediate results when we spend our time, say, building a brand, creating a website, and publishing on social media. It might feel like focusing our energies and attention on our course of action is more beneficial than talking to God—something that does not display instant, measurable, and visible results—but taking courses of action apart from prayer is trusting in ourselves as opposed to trusting our Creator.

Another temptation that keeps us from praying is due to how easy it is to turn to others for advice about our situations. With the touch of a button we have the ability to connect with others via text, phone call, or video chat. Search engines and online forums add to our list of go-to resources. We vent, complain, and seek advice, hoping for that "ah-ha!" moment or the missing puzzle piece to our dilemma. In our attempt to find a quick fix, we disregard the all-wise and all-knowing One who has all authority and power. Our urgency to find an answer feels so pressing that an in-the-flesh response may appear to offer more comfort than set apart time spent on our knees waiting on the Lord. (As an aside, we are also quick to give advice to vulnerable advice-seekers. We would do well to ask if the one seeking advice has taken this to the Lord first, and if not, then the time spent together starts with prayer.) Philippians 4:6–7 says, "Don't worry about anything, but in everything, through prayer and petition with thanksgiving, present your requests to God. And the peace of God, which surpasses all understanding, will guard your hearts and minds in Christ Jesus." It's important to seek counsel and do our due diligence to help inform our decision, but ultimately the woman with a dream should be less concerned with casting her cares and burdens on others and more concerned with laying them down before the Lord. Having a dream isn't wrong, but entrusting it to people instead of God most certainly is.

A truly heart-felt prayer requires time, thought, and discipline. Picture the growth of a flower. Rain falls onto the ground and nourishes the seed. That seed grows and blooms into a beautiful flower. With petals in full bloom, that flower faces upward and looks to both the sun and rain for its vitality. If God's Word is the rain that falls upon us, prayer is the flower turned upward to the Sun. It depends on and acknowledges its source of life. Scripture reading and prayer are intertwined. Our knowledge of and love for the Lord overflows into our prayer life. Prayer is not a power move—it's a move of humility. And it is a divine mandate that calls us to remain in a continual spirit of prayer throughout our days (1 Thess. 5:17). This doesn't mean we pray through our order at the drive-through or while scheduling appointments on the phone (though, we totally can do that), but it does mean we make it a part of our lifestyle. Jesus was the perfect example of this. As we read throughout the Gospels, we see that He intentionally carved out time to pray.

- "After dismissing the crowds, he went up on the mountain by himself *to pray*. Well into the night, he was there alone" (Matt. 14:23, emphasis added).
- "Very early in the morning, while it was still dark, he got up, went out, and made his way to a deserted place; and *there he was praying*" (Mark 1:35, emphasis added).

- "... *he was praying* in private ..." (Luke 9:18, emphasis added).
- "*He was praying* in a certain place, and when he finished, one of his disciples said to him, 'Lord, teach us to pray ...'" (Luke 11:1, emphasis added).

And, of course, the most fervent of all of Jesus' prayers was in the Garden of Gethsemane just before His death: "Being in anguish, he prayed more fervently, and his sweat became like drops of blood falling to the ground" (Luke 22:44). If Jesus Himself prayed without ceasing, so should His followers. This, too, is abiding in the Lord and the result of seeking God in prayer will not only assist in the putting off of the works of the flesh but will naturally yield fruit in our lives.

Prayer takes our head knowledge and converts it into heart knowledge. The dreamer that occupies her mind and her time with prayer is one that isn't running around fretting about future decisions. She is a humble woman who recognizes Who it is that holds her in His hands and she is willing to entrust her dream with Him. She is at peace and remains confident that the Lord hears her and will answer her prayer according to His will and perfect plans.

3. The Church

Jesus is the bridegroom and the church is His bride (Eph. 5: Rev. 19:7). He gave Himself up for her, imperfect as she may be right now (Eph. 5:25). We are a part of the greater Church (with a big C), and our love for the overflow into our local churches (little c). However, the thought of "church" may unearth a wide variety of feelings for some. There are many—myself included—who have a history of painful experiences with other Christians and whole congregations. There may be residual pain or bitterness making it hard to commit to a church body. Oftentimes, we find a place that seems wonderful but then as we grow closer to the people within that church body, we discover it to be just as broken as a previous place. Many move from church to church while others give up on it altogether, determining that their own personal study and prayer time is enough.

I cannot defend every church. There are many today who do not cling to sound doctrine and the result of that is all sorts of quarrels and divisions within church bodies that reflect a model contrary to what the Lord calls the Church to reflect. Sometimes the pain inflicted upon attendees stems from a deeper-rooted issue within those church bodies. This is why Paul spent so much time addressing the early church, confronting them with their twisted versions of the gospel and gospel living.

But here's the thing: if Paul gave up on every church that had its issues, there would be no churches worth writing to or praying over as he did. He loved the Church deeply because God loves the Church deeply. This is why Paul wrote with such fervor, zeal, and passion. He loved them and longed for them to grow in holiness. There are still churches in existence that for all their problems, they really do faithfully proclaim the Word, cling to sound doctrine, and try their best to live it out. Jesus did not come to call the righteous, but the sinners; therefore, our churches are filled with imperfect people who are also battling the flesh.

God set up this system for a reason. He desires us to walk alongside one another, not tolerating one another's sin but confessing it to one another, encouraging repentance, stirring one another up in love and good works, implementing church discipline, and forgiving one another as Jesus has forgiven us. So, while I never want to minimize or dismiss whatever hardship another believer has walked through, I also cannot minimize or dismiss the fact that God's plan for His people includes the Church. After all, Jesus died for the Church. He's not ever going to give up on it, and neither should we.

The Christian dreamer loves and values the Church. Through the accountability and support of local leadership and likeminded believers, she has a wealth of wisdom and support to draw from. She understands that being an active participant in her church community is another vital way to cultivate the soil of her heart so that she will bear fruit and spur others to do the same. The preaching and teaching of the Word, the corporate singing and praying to God, and the bearing of burdens are all formative things that happen in the context of local church life, and are the very things that help the dreamer remain steadfast amidst the craziness of life, prioritizing first things first.

Let me just take a quick moment to say this: if part of our dream in this life has nothing to do with building up Christ's bride in regular and sacrificial ways, rest assured our dream and God's will are at odds. Far too many "important Christian people" get away with not laboring on the local level while demanding that their dream take them to a national or international level of influence. There could be nothing worse for both that particular dreamer as well as all those they are influencing. If your dream takes you away from local church community or requires you to take unusually long seasons of absence from laboring amidst the people in your immediate proximity, you've missed the whole point of not just dreaming, but the Christian life.

If we want to be fruitful Christians, it's vital that we plug in to a solid, trust-worthy Church body that glorifies God, clings to the Word, edifies its congregants, devotes themselves to fellowship, and makes disciples of all nations. Dreams and the success of dreams can be fun, but they also fade—but praise be to Jesus, the Church will remain both now and into eternity as Christ's bride.

Fruit Born over Time

A few years ago, our family faced another deployment that would take my husband away for several months. Ethan left right after our Cora's two-month birthday, and I was on my own during those newborn months. There were many opportunities for me to neglect time in the Word, time in prayer, and time spent at church. It was up to me whether or not I would discipline myself to abide in Jesus. Ethan was gone, and my kids were certainly not going to walk with God for me.

It was so much more convenient to skip the midweek Bible study or Sunday morning service and avoid getting three kids ready and out the door. But I had gone through enough deployments to know that I needed an anchor in the midst of a season that could easily toss me to and fro. I didn't want to be the bitter wife I once was who completely missed out on the spiritual growth and vital lessons that God offers in the midst of hard seasons. And so, I pulled out my Bible in between naps and late at night. I spoke (and sometimes cried) prayers out loud in the living room on the couch where Ethan and I would normally sit in the evenings. I loaded my kids in the car and headed to church Sunday after Sunday to not only be filled myself, but to fill my kids as well.

And over time, by the grace of God and the power of the Holy Spirit, I bore fruit in a season where I normally would have withered. The Dianne from years prior would've grumbled and complained when that winter storm hit us hard and I was outside shoveling three feet of snow on my own. The Dianne I knew would have lost her mind when she walked into her three-year-old's room to find permanent marker all over the bed, toys, and walls in her rental home. But the Dianne of that season didn't do those things, and *that was supernatural.* And on days when I felt weaker, the Lord provided—not just through my local church but from other Christians who are part of the big "C" Church. One new friend dropped off burritos so I wouldn't have to make dinner. Another teacher came by with his son and son's friend to shovel the rest of our driveway. My Lola (the Filipino word for grandma) flew out and stayed with me to help with my newborn. A Christian preschool attached to our church at that time was fully booked, but created two openings and offered a scholarship to make room for Kaiden and Skye so that I could have a few hours of a break twice a week. God met our needs in great abundance that season. And after that deployment, my husband came home to a changed woman—freed from the need to compare roles, and freed from high expectations. Instead he found a woman filled with the fruit of the Spirit, thanks be to God.

I don't share that in pride. I share that to tell you that God really *can* change things. He really can change *you*. By the power of the Holy Spirit you have every ability to bear fruit in seasons of confusion or difficulty. I know having a hard time and commiserating about the hardship is the easier road to take. I get that memes and blogs about the challenges of motherhood and work and life are funny and sometimes refreshingly real. But those things won't change you. They may make you feel understood, and that surely has a place, but they can also sometimes reinforce the idea that you'll always be this way. That hard day with the kids will always feel this hard. That annoying task you had to do will always be done in frustration. The obsession you have about your dream will always grip you to this level of suffocation. But that's not the truth. The truth is, God is able to move in you. God is able to make you different. God is able to change the way you perceive and respond to your day. He is able to change the way you view, engage in, and strategize everything, even your dream. God *really is* able to move in your heart in this area. He's that good.

The Fruitful Dreamer

If we are going to be dreamers and doers, we better be fruitful ones, because apart from abiding in the True Vine, there are so many opportunities for the works of the flesh to manifest themselves. We will be like the dead branches that are tossed aside and burnt up. Jesus says, "You are the salt of the earth. But if the salt should lose its taste, how can it be made salty? It's no longer good for anything but to be thrown out and trampled under people's feet" (Matt. 5:13). Salt provides distinctness and flavor. Loss of that flavor is useless. When we bear fruit, we prove ourselves to be set apart, to be salt and light in this confusing, sin-stained world.

The dreamer that walks in step with the Spirit is a fruitful Christian. She exudes joy, waits on the Lord patiently, and does not live a life of selfish ambition in her pursuit of whatever calling is impressed on her heart. She recognizes that her ability to bear any sort of virtue is rooted in her walk with the Lord and she uses the God-given tools like Bible reading, prayer, and her local church as a means of pursuing a virtuous and holy lifestyle. She abides in Jesus and He in her with the end goal that she will inherit the kingdom of God. The fruit she bears testifies to the God she loves, and that is a reputation every dreamer should be known for.

I know the previous paragraph might sound like a laundry list of things you'll never be. It used to sound that way to me too. But hear me: it's possible. It really is possible. God can really make you into this kind of dreamer—one able to handle the ups and downs that inevitably come with our dreams, free of bitterness, resentment, comparison, and every other work of the flesh. Walking in the Spirit, abiding in Christ, putting off the old self—these things really can change the entire way you walk through the dream-chasing experience, and more than that, they can change the way you walk through every experience. God can do it. He can change you. He can bear fruit in your heart. He is able. Do you believe that?

Chapter 6

YOU AREN'T FILLER

"Our work for Christ is not passive; it demands sacrifice, planning, energy, wisdom, and passion. Nevertheless, all of that effort is futile unless Christ remains the source of strength powerfully at work in our inner being."[1]

—Dr. Glenn Jago

A few summers ago, I attended a Christian women's conference. My friend Beatrice and I happened to stay at the hotel where all the speakers of that event stayed. There were a few times we shared elevators with some of the keynote speakers or worship leaders we saw up on stage. I thought back to my Jasmine Star moment: "Oh, how starstruck I was then. She is just a person. These are just people. I've really grown since then." Right after the conference ended, I walked toward the front desk to check out of our hotel. It was then I saw John Piper—a pastor, author, and man of God whom I deeply admire—standing in the lobby across from me. He had just finished preaching the last keynote message and was clearly exhausted and in need of rest. But that didn't stop Beatrice and me from rushing up to him to say hello and thank him for his ministry.

After a brief exchange of words, he walked away and I quickly blurted out, "Can we please get a picture with you?" He must not have heard me because he kept walking. Another group of women swarmed him outside and I watched as they snapped a selfie with him. I had a split-second decision to make. Do I chase after him and try to take my own selfie or do I let him go? By this point, he had already moved his wife's bags into their rental car. We didn't want to bother him once more. I grabbed my friend and we decided to take a selfie through the window with him in the background. We needed proof that we bumped into John Piper because if we didn't document it, it didn't happen, right? Just as we snapped the picture, he turned his head away and all we could see in the image was our giddy faces and a blur of a man that could have been anyone. We laughed about it and then I thought, *I think this is the way it's supposed to be. John Piper would have wanted it this way.*

Afterward, when I really thought about the purpose of this photo, what it boiled down to was bragging rights. It wasn't enough that I heard him speak on a stage from a few hundred feet away. (I'm pretty sure I snapped a picture of him on stage too.) No, a picture of us side-by-side would have revealed actual one-on-one interaction. But if you know anything about him and his ministry, John Piper doesn't preach to make John Piper known; he preaches to make God's name known. I'm certain that he would rather me post about the object of his message—God Himself—or what the Lord taught me through his message, rather than who I heard the message from. You see, like the elevator faces and like you and me, John Piper is just a person also walking in obedience to what God has called him to. He might be categorized as a celebrity pastor by some (okay, by *me* in that moment), but really he was formerly a sinner in need of Jesus just as much as we all are. He and I read the same Bible, and he is filled with the same Holy Spirit that fills me. While there's nothing wrong with admiring a person's faith and following in their example, the reality is that John Piper is no greater than I. As the saying goes, the ground is level at the foot of the cross.

Unfortunately, Christian circles are guilty of placing certain roles within the Church on a pedestal. We have a slew of celebrity pastors, authors, and musicians that, sadly, are worshiped by their followers.

While some fans may be guilty of idolizing these "super-Christians," there are also those Christian celebrities who parade themselves and act as though their talent or success within their medium is their own when, in reality, they abuse the very gift that God has given them to use for His glory. They may give a semblance of being God-glorifying, but deep within their heart they are inwardly focused. They are dream-chasers, their dream being an elevated sense of self and a bunch of fans to affirm that sense. While pursuit and ambition aren't always wrong, they are going about these things for all the wrong reasons.

Think I'm being harsh? Consider the Pharisees whose outward life projected a life of holiness while inwardly they were the furthest thing from holy. If not careful, this mentality can easily be found in our local churches or "online ministries" where mini-kingdoms are built amongst church staff, worship teams, Christian influencers, or deep-pocketed attendees as the center. This attitude is the total opposite of how Paul conducted himself in life and ministry. He makes it clear in 1 Thessalonians 2 that a worker approved by God doesn't share the gospel to please man, receive words of flattery, or serve for financial gain. Paul makes it clear that his work was never from a motive of glory-seeking, even though as traveling apostles they could have easily made many requests to their benefit.

The reality is that the issue of special treatment within Christianity isn't new. James addresses the sin of partiality:

> My brothers and sisters, do not show favoritism as you hold on to the faith in our glorious Lord Jesus Christ. For if someone comes into your meeting wearing a gold ring and dressed in fine clothes, and a poor person dressed in filthy clothes also comes in, if you look with favor on the one wearing the fine clothes and say, "Sit here in a good place," and yet you say to the poor person, "Stand over there," or "Sit here on the floor by my footstool," haven't you made

> distinctions among yourselves and become judges with evil thoughts? (James 2:1–4)

James knew that elevating others on the basis of outward appearance (or in our context, any reason for that matter) is a problem. He made it clear that the Church has no room for this kind of favoritism. When we elevate anyone for worldly reasons—whether the rich man for his fine clothing or the pastor for his ability to get congregants to open their pockets or the worship singer for her attractiveness—we walk in the spirit of the world and we damage a biblical view of God-given gifts and roles within the Church.

When we measure greatness by earthly standards, not only do we skew our entire view of the Church, but we distort the importance of the role we play in it. In sinfully elevating the John Pipers of Christianity, the default is the demoting of ourselves and everyone around us.

I long for women to see that every single woman around them is worth knowing and loving: the root of my admiration is the women in their small group, the individuals in their workplace, the neighbors in their community, as well as the woman looking in their mirror. I do understand. The way I respect and admire John Piper naturally makes me want to be in his presence, but the root of my admiration is Christ in John Piper. What we're after is Jesus.

I can't speak for everyone, but in the dream-chasing space, I think a lot of us are hoping, wishing, and waiting for our time to shine. We may not want front-and-center spotlight (though some of us might), but we want to make our mark on the world. We want to do the *big* things for God and wonder if He has some *special* calling on our lives. This leaves many doubting themselves, believing that He has only assigned that *special* calling for others. Someone once wrote me and questioned whether she is just "extra filler" in God's plan. This could not be further from the truth and yet, it is a commonly held belief among many who feel like there is no real purpose in their lives currently.

We must understand that every ministry, every talent, every spiritual gift is given from God and should be offered for God. Spiritual gifts are specific Holy Spirit-given gifts distributed to the believer after salvation. These are different from natural talents, though their uses point to the same end. First Corinthians 12:4–6 says: "Now there are different gifts, but the *same* Spirit. There are different ministries, but the *same* Lord. And there are different activities, but the *same* God produces each gift in each person." Do you see the word *same* in there three times? We all have different gifts, ministries, and activities, but the common denominator is God. It's not about us and who is doing what and how amazing they are doing it. He is the one handing out the assignments and His holy purposes all point back to Him!

Verse 11 confirms the pattern we see of the "same Spirit," "same Lord," and "same God" when it says: "One and the same Spirit is active in all these, distributing to each person as he wills." The Christian life isn't an episode of *Oprah* where everyone in the audience "wins" the same gift. In His kindness and creativity, He entrusts each of us with different ways of serving Him. We get different gifts, and we use those gifts in different ways, in different roles, and at different times, our dreams included. Our gifts were never meant to be showy displays that shout, "Look at me!" God's intention in giving the gifts was never about the gifts themselves or elevating the recipients' status, but rather helping the Church body function as He intended it to. The goal of the gifts is to build up the *body*, not the gifted.

Scripture continues as it focuses in on the importance of the Church body and its collective parts: "For just as the body is one and has many parts, and all the parts of that body, though many, are one body—so also is Christ. For we were all baptized by one Spirit into one body—whether Jews or Greeks, whether slaves or free—and we were all given one Spirit to drink" (1 Cor. 12:12–13).

Back to my John Piper example: I am not John Piper and John Piper is not me, but we were both baptized by one Spirit into the same body. How cool that he is my spiritual brother along with countless other brothers whose names I do not yet know? So, when Paul says "Whether Jews or Greeks, whether slaves or free . . ." we see how we can welcome both the rich man and the poor man into our churches knowing that their outward appearances, social statuses, or any other detail of their lives matters not because we have the same Spirit. Each part of the body is equally vital and valuable:

> Indeed, the body is not one part but many. If the foot should say, "Because I'm not a hand, I don't belong to the body," it is not for that reason any less a part of the body. And if the ear should say, "Because I'm not an eye, I don't belong to the body," it is not for that reason any less a part of the body. If the whole body were an eye, where would the hearing be? If the whole body were an ear, where would the sense of smell be? (1 Cor. 12:14–17)

Consider the knee I mentioned earlier that I injured after slipping on the stairs: it's a vital part of my body if I want to run, jump, or even walk. I put makeup on my face, and I dress my torso, but I can't say I ever showcase or pay much attention to my knees. Does this make my knee any less important? Scripture defends the ear, the eye, the nose, and the rest of us. "If the whole body were an ear, where would the sense of smell be?"

If we were all worship leaders, who would teach? Who would pour into the nursery kids? Who would welcome old and new attendees—literally, one of the first impressions of the entire church? Your church may not have all the theatrics or world's best coffee, but by the power of the Holy Spirit, one friendly face from a greeter can soften the heart of someone who needs to sit in those pews and hear the gospel. Each member in the church has an important and unique role to play.

While some roles are more up front and others are behind the scenes, no one is insignificant. All are needed and everyone matters.

Though these passages are clearly referencing the Church, the principles apply to the dreamer. Just as the church in Corinth tended to elevate and idolize certain leaders and gifts, so does the world, and sadly, so does the general Christian market—whether that be the worship music industry, the world of Instagram and blogs, the podcast dynasties, the conference circuit, and so on. So many women are trying to get their season of fame in one of these spheres of influence, and they call it godliness. And worse, they think if they don't, they are just filler. They don't matter. Their lives aren't impressive enough. They haven't made their mark. This kind of thinking is foreign to historical Christianity, which were primarily ordinary people whose names and faithfulness we may never know. In fact, seasons of influence and power are actually things the Bible tells us to be incredibly wary of, for many of those wrapped up in these things will not enter God's kingdom.

God arranged each one of the parts in the Church body (and each person in each industry—whatever industry you may be dreaming about) just as He wanted. Possessing gifts or talents isn't like an Easter egg hunt where all the church members start in the same place, hunting around the church attempting to find the biggest, shiniest egg with the best prize inside. Paul saw fit to mention yet again that it is God who is behind the scenes orchestrating things as He wills. Our envy of each other's gifts, natural abilities, positions, influence, and life-callings calls God's purpose into question. When we determine that someone else has it better—better looks, better calling, better network, better income, better marriage, better gifting, and so on, we really take on a sense of entitlement, assuming God has somehow short-changed us in this life. The fact of the matter is that we did nothing to earn these gifts or position in the world. While many try to fake a calling or giftedness or position, the truth is, God decides who goes where and how they are wired. We just don't get to control that, and when we try to, we are miserable. In the same way that God designed your eye and skin color, so you received your gifts as He chose to offer them to you.

This reminds me of a tough but true phrase my son once heard from a teacher: *You get what you get, and you don't get upset.* Kaiden hates that he shared this with me because I definitely use it when I'm distributing unequally cut brownies or am assigning house chores to him and his sisters. Of course, God doesn't desire a "suck it up" attitude. While, yes, God will distribute the gifts and callings and experiences He sees fit to dole out to each of us, He's not doing it arbitrarily. He desires us to trust that He knows best, and what He's given us is actually and truly *good* for us. In fact, it's what we would ask Him to give us if we knew everything He did! This is faith—believing and rejoicing in that whatever He has chosen to give us really is the best plan. Each Christian already has the gift of salvation, and now we have Spirit-empowered abilities to serve the Church and the greater Christian community in our own unique capacity, in our unique seasons, and in our own unique communities! In fact, we should rejoice that we are not all the same:

> And if they were all the same part, where would the body be? As it is, there are many parts, but one body. The eye cannot say to the hand, "I don't need you!" Or again, the head can't say to the feet, "I don't need you!" On the contrary, those parts of the body that are weaker are indispensable. And those parts of the body that we consider less honorable, we clothe these with greater honor, and our unrespectable parts are treated with greater respect, which our respectable parts do not need. (1 Cor. 12:19–24)

Paul wrote to a people who over-valued their gifts so much that they felt they could do without the rest of the Church body. And yet, he affirms that even the weaker or less honorable portions (such as the organs, completely internal and unseen) are indispensable.

The theme we see here is that all are essential. We are all created to do good works (Eph. 2:10). "And he himself gave some to be apostles, some prophets, some evangelists, some pastors and teachers, equipping the saints for the work of ministry, to build up the body of Christ, until we all reach unity in the faith and in the knowledge of God's Son, growing into maturity with a stature measured by Christ's fullness" (Eph. 4:11–13). The hand isn't better than the organs, and the organs are not better than the hand. In God's creativity, He offered diversity to aid in church unity and maturity.

We may cringe at the snowflake mantra of teachers these days: "Every one of my students is special." But the reality is that each Christian really is unique in function. Comprehending the importance of the Church body changes everything for the Christian who feels others have been designated a special calling or who view themselves as "filler." God assigned you a unique and particular role within His grand story. He tailored your life in a divine way to fit into the greater body and glorify Him (1 Cor. 12:7). Both the Communion cup collector and the announcement-giver, and both the preacher and the worship leader belong to the same body, and together they collectively honor the same God. No one is filler.

Gifts for the Glory of God and the Benefit of Others

Imagine someone entrusting you with a blank check to use in service to your neighbor down the street who desperately needs the help. This single mom of two just lost her job and is struggling to make ends meet. Not only can she not afford to pay for childcare for her youngest, but school just let out and her bills increase as she needs childcare for two. You glance out your window and notice her exit her car with hands full—diaper bag and child on one hip, and stack of job applications in the other hand. Now let's say that instead of assisting in meeting their needs, you decide to take that check to the nearest Anthropology clothing store and spend it all on yourself. This would be considered a selfish act and an abuse of the gift, right? Similarly, God distributes gifts with the intention that they be used to love those around us. They were not given for our own personal benefit or self-promotion. "Just as each one has received a gift, use it to serve others, as good stewards of the varied grace of God" (1 Pet. 4:10). To steward something is to manage it well. If we want to be a good steward, we will stop looking to ourselves and start looking at the needs of those around us. Think about your own gifts or dreams. How do they serve other people? Who have they served recently? In what ways? Can you list any specifics? If not, your gifts and your dreams, though baptized in Christian-speak, may just be about you.

I doubt there is any church or ministry that can say, "All our needs are met." Most churches have a shortage of volunteers and desperately need help for work that the church staff simply cannot cover. My question is: Are we overlooking opportunities to serve around us because we are too fixated on the dreams we have for ourselves? It's hard to imagine one more thing added to our plates and yet this is one of *the* things God requires of Christians. It's not a question of whether or not we should do it. The reality is black-and-white: If we love God, we will love our neighbor too, and that includes serving others through our God-given gifts and talents in the Church body. This is "faith working through love" (Gal. 5:6). Think about it. If your dreams and giftedness prevent you from serving the ordinary people in your own neighborhood or church, can you say you're using them for the right reasons? If you want to influence many online but you're not actually laboring in your local church, if ministering to a handful of women in your neighborhood seems beneath you, if ten sounds boring but ten thousand sounds intoxicating, why should anyone follow you as an example? You'll lead them right into *not* serving their church, into *not* following the pattern for influence Jesus clearly exhibits in the Gospels, where He invests in a few instead of the crowds.

Paul stands as a wonderful example of a man who used his gifts to build up the body of Christ and serve others instead of focusing on himself or building some sort of personal kingdom or platform. All of his epistles display his clear affection for *the people he shepherded*—not his position or his gifting—as seen in his thanksgiving and prayers for the church. He encourages us in Galatians 6:10 (ESV), "As we have opportunity, let us do good to everyone . . ." This isn't a "I have to" but an "I get to!" When we serve our neighbor in love, we are loving our neighbor as ourselves and we are presenting ourselves as a "living sacrifice, holy and pleasing to God" (Rom. 12:1).

How exciting that God saw fit to give each of us a specific gift and to form in us specific talents and abilities that will build up others around us! Rather than looking around longingly at what everyone else is doing (which is comparison, discontent, and selfish ambition), we are free to step into the role He saw fit to place us in. We cheer on our brothers and sisters in their various callings because we understand Who their gifts are from and Who they point back to. If God gave them that, then praise be to God, for He knows what He's doing and what He's doing is good.

I'm amazed when I consider the various men and women that I've come across using their God-given gifts for His glory. My sweet friend Josi has the gift of teaching and hospitality and has a heart for people in general. In her season of singleness, she spent several years living and teaching English in Asia, but her primary aim was to lead her students to the Lord. Now that she is a mom and pastor's wife living in California, she continues to utilize those gifts in a new capacity. Another friend, Hunter, is a beautiful mom of three who loves her kids dearly. From the moment I met her in a church Bible study, her gifts of speaking, teaching, and explaining complex truths in a simple way were obvious to all. Not only is she a faithful leader in her church and military community, but she also operates her side-hustle

Journeywomen podcast, while her kids are in bed and right out of her closet. Her love for the Lord is consistent across the board whether in parenting, reaching out to her community, or encouraging women internationally.

And then there is Josh, whom I met in college. He has the gift of evangelism, and I will never forget him preaching messages in chapel and rounding us students up to go out into the city and evangelize to the lost around us. To this day he and his wife faithfully share the gospel with all he encounters whether on the street, in a coffee shop, or within his home. He has led many people to the Lord and encouraged many Christians to remain faithful in their call to discipleship.

All three of these people know from Whom their gifts come and all three give their gifts right back to Him. And the beauty of it all is that the ability to use their gifts hasn't changed as their seasons of life changed. And that is the truth for us too. Maybe you're a working woman, with a deep love for kids and a unique ability to paint, but your current job doesn't make room for either of those skill sets. Consider volunteering to watch another mom's kids and teach them how to paint while you're there. Or see if you can work those gifts into VBS at your church. Or perhaps you're a widow with a passion for prayer and a love for hospitality. Invite someone over for coffee and offer to pray for them, or bring hospitality to their door and pray for them at their doorstep. Whatever it is that God has entrusted you with, get creative and start dreaming up the ways you can use those giftings right now. Let me say it again: you aren't filler. Your gifts were given to you right where you are to be used for someone right in front of you, right where they are.

Practically speaking, the ordinary callings of our lives don't always feel glamorous. If feelings were a barometer for our value of service to God, in my limited experience, the routine callings before me would appear to fall short of ministry or creative ventures every single time. But the beauty of God's mysterious ways is that even these ordinary moments are injected with purpose. The gospel can be proclaimed, discipleship can happen, and the Church can be built up not just in the form of a magazine or ministry but within the walls of our homes—possibly even more so within our homes because it's a daily pouring into those around us as opposed to words on a page published seasonally. Michael Horton addresses this:

> It is all too easy to turn other people in our lives into a supporting cast for our life movie. The problem is that they don't follow the role or the lines we've given them. They are actual people with actual needs that get in the way of our plot, especially if they're as ambitious as we are. Sometimes, chasing your dreams can be "easier" than just being who we are, where God has placed you, with the gifts he has given to you.[2]

He's right. Sometimes it can be much easier to create or write or serve or work or minister to other women "out there" than to labor in love toward those "in here," like our own parents, neighbors, roommates, friends, siblings, husband, or kids. My kids are not the supporting cast in my personal life movie. But when we are gripped by a future dream, how easy is it for us to view present commitments—in my case, my children—as a hindrance to that dream? The very notion that my calling as a wife and mom (and the ordinary tasks that come with it) are of lesser value than the outside work I do is a complete lie. I may see some immediate fruit in the thing I love to do (ministering to women), and you may see some good and valid fruit from the things you love to do, but if you are married with kids, let me tell you something: loving our husbands, growing and discipling little souls from the ground up, and investing in our homes is a mighty task—a biblical task (Titus 2)! It's not less than or second best. Kingdom work begins with loving the Lord your God with all your heart, soul, and mind in your own heart and home, and then overflows to your neighbors around you.

Understanding our calling within the Church transforms our view of our day-to-day. No longer is life "wash, rinse, repeat." It's an opportunity to glorify God in all that we do. "So, whether you eat or drink, or whatever you do, do everything for the glory of God" (1 Cor. 10:31). We eat three times a day at a minimum. It's a cyclical task. It happens over and over and over again. Like the careless prayer we can easily throw out before a meal, how often do we engage in eating without even giving God's glory a thought? And yet Paul says, we must do it to the glory of God. This poses the question: Have we even considered that the mundane moments are opportunities to ascribe glory to God? Or have we separated these routine habits and reserved our time with the Lord only for morning devotions, midweek Bible study, or Sunday church?

Just imagine. Even the very act of breathing can give God glory! How? God is the One who gives us life and who sustains us (Gen. 2:7; Isa. 42:5; Job 12:10). When we consider the fact that the breath you and I are taking right now is God-given and yet totally undeserved, it leads us to a spirit of praise. Psalm 150:6 says: "Let everything that breathes praise the Lord. Hallelujah!" The one who gives God glory in all that he or she does has a conscious reliance upon God. Whether we breathe, blink, serve others, or dream, the possibilities for glorying God in our ordinary moments are endless.

I love how one pastor writes to our restless generation:

> What we need are fewer revolutionaries and a few more plodding visionaries. . . . The best churches are full of gospel-saturated people holding tenaciously to a vision of godly obedience and God's glory, and pursuing that godliness and glory with relentless, often unnoticed, plodding consistency. . . . Daily discipleship is not a new revolution each morning or

> an agent of global transformation every evening; it's a long obedience in the same direction.[3]

The dreamer's pursuit must remain fixated on God's glory, and the means by which that happens is faithful obedience through the help of the Holy Spirit over the long haul. The stepping-stones to getting there will surely look different for everyone, but they are always moving away from ourselves and this world and closer to our God and His glory.

It is here we must ask ourselves: Why are we pursuing our dreams? Is it really to do great things for God? Is it really because God called us to do this? Do these dreams fit into the mission of giving Him glory and loving our neighbors? Do they offer us opportunity to build up the Church? Or do they tempt us to assume the ordinary people in our lives are beneath us?

When we truly seek God's will and missional purpose in our lives, there will be contentment in everyday moments because of the knowledge that He is also glorified in the unseen details of our day. When we recognize that the Lord has gifted us each individually to function within the greater Church body for His ultimate glory, it is there we may find contentment.

No longer do you need to look side to side, envious of someone else's calling or fixated on how you can elevate your own. No longer are you bound by numbers and status and what's visibly noticed by others. What God has entrusted you with is no better and no less important than what He has chosen for your other brothers and sisters in Christ. We can rejoice in each other's accomplishments and successes because we share in the same Spirit and have been offered the same salvation, which is more than enough. But know that you are uniquely gifted and you play an important role in the Church body. How has the Lord gifted you? What areas of your life are you incredibly passionate about and in what ways can you use those abilities to serve others immediately around you? Look at the needs around you and start dreaming up the ways He may be calling you to meet those needs. Get out of agreement with the idea that you're just filler, and start using what God has planted in you for others and for Himself.

Chapter 7

THE CHRISTIAN DREAMER'S SECRET WEAPON

"We ourselves are 'saved to save'—we are made to give—to let everything go if only we may have more to give. The pebble takes in the rays of light that fall on it, but the diamond flashes them out again: every little facet is means, not simply of drinking more in, but of giving more out."[1]

—I. Lilias Trotter

Most of the dreams penned and hidden in the folds of my notebook occurred to me during naptime. I did not have the time or the luxury to browse museums for inspiration or sit in coffee shops and think. My dreams had to take place in the window between playtime and afternoon snack. It was the summer of 2013, and we were expecting baby number two. A very pregnant me in need of a few minutes to catch my breath sat on our living room couch, mindlessly scrolling on Instagram. An online friend posted a beautiful, flat-lay image of her new copy of an independent magazine. I hadn't seen anything like it before.

The magazine had a clean design, beautiful imagery, and it's popularity spread across the hipster community like wildfire for these very reasons. The concept was simple: a trendy magazine with articles about gathering together through food and community. The ad-free content and film-like photos printed on high-quality paper were stunning—even through the vantage point of a cell phone screen. I began poring over their website, and I grew fascinated over this unique product. There was no Kim Kardashian on the cover. It didn't have giant, bright font with "10 Tips to Win Him Back." No newsstand magazine could compare to this.

About a week or more later, the copy I ordered for myself arrived. I carefully opened up the cardboard box and pulled out the magazine, hand-wrapped in white butcher paper. It's cover was protected with an aqueous coating that was soft to the touch. Its pages were not thin and glossy like traditional magazines, they were matte-like and sturdy. The magazine was heavy, weighing about one pound, and the quality of it felt more like a book than a magazine.

I waited until Kaiden's next naptime to sit and read it. From a photographer's standpoint, this was incredible; but from a Christian perspective, it was lacking. Though it was beautiful and set apart from most traditional magazines, worldly wisdom still permeated all of the advice offered or suggestions made. The more I read, the more sadness I felt that their attempt at achieving joy was through minimalism, authenticity, hospitality, and good food. The magazine lacked because it lacked God at the center of it all—the reason for living intentionally, sharing and enjoying good food and company. Their attempt at hospitality wasn't a bad thing, but they were missing the God who is hospitable to us all in Christ—the One who created hospitality in the first place. And that is when the idea for a Christian women's magazine formed in my mind.

So many Christians that I followed on Instagram posted about their copies of the magazine. Clearly, print is not dead. What if there was a magazine similar to this in look, feel, and design, but was rooted in glorifying God? What if we could encourage women in sound doctrine through the form of a magazine? What if we could share how the gospel impacts our work, our cooking, our schedules, our homes, our marriages, our ministries, our friendships, our kids, and our day-to-day living?

I put my search engine to work and began looking around to see if a product like this already existed. There were a few Christian magazines on the market, but they looked nothing like what I was envisioning, nor did they contain the type of content I was hoping to curate. There was a gap that needed filling.

This new dream would allow me to use my photography, and would also satisfy my desire to spiritually encourage other women. I knew I could not do this alone, and it thrilled me to think that this would allow other men and women to step in and use their gifts too!

I pulled out my crumpled, floral notebook. Sandwiched between other pages with other dreams, I began scribbling ideas down for this magazine. I filled those pages with name ideas, the purpose and mission, and first-issue article ideas. I eagerly shared the idea when Ethan arrived home but we both agreed that the birth of our second child should remain first priority for now. In the meantime, he encouraged me to pray about it and gather more information on what it would take for this magazine idea to actually happen.

Press Pause

It wasn't long after that conversation that we finally received our new duty station assignment: Fort Benning, Georgia. Just one month before our move date, I gave birth to Skye. This new season of life meant that the magazine was an idea that we would have to press pause on. It remained hidden in my notebook, buried under packing paper and tucked away in one of dozens of moving boxes. I was at peace. Right now, our family was in transition and this dream would have to wait.

Sometimes, keeping our dreams on paper and filed away in our mind is the best way to determine whether or not we are totally invested in it. It's easy to be fired up about a new venture, but it's in the praying and waiting that we really discover if our desire to pursue it is simply excitement as opposed to a calling. Looking back, I'm thankful that the answer from God in this season regarding my dream wasn't a yes or a no per se, but a "pause."

In the meantime, our movers picked up 90 percent of our belongings. We kept the remaining 10 percent and journeyed across the country in our travel-trailer. Ethan took off work and for two months we soaked up all the firsts with our newborn while slowly journeying across the country. We camped out in the California desert. We took a last-minute detour to the Grand Canyon. We stayed with friends in New Mexico, broke down in Texas, and spent a few weeks with family in Oklahoma. And when we finally made it to Georgia, we lived in that twenty-five-foot camper for another month and a half until our home was move-in ready. All throughout this time, the idea to start this magazine steeped in the back of my mind and in the depths of my heart.

Rather than impatience, there was contentment. Rather than comparison, there was joy.

What mattered in these moments was acclimating our family to the new area. We stumbled upon CrossPointe Church in Columbus, Georgia. If I had a time line for my Christian journey, this wonderful place would be yet another important marker. I came just in time to sign up for their first women's Systematic Theology 101 class. This course changed everything for me. I grew to understand the value of theological education in the Church, and as I studied, my eyes opened to the various attributes of God and doctrinal themes woven throughout Scripture that I hadn't seen before.

Our class was full. Women of all ages were hungry for the Word and deeper truths about God. Unlike some studies that focus more on experience, feelings, and how this relates to *me*, this course centered on the Word of God, *His* character throughout biblical history, and by knowing Him more, we learned what the Christian's response is in all of this life. By the end of the course, the desire to start this magazine grew stronger than ever before.

One day after Bible study, I went onto a crowdfunding website. (Crowdfunding websites, if you aren't familiar, are spaces where people with ideas create campaigns to raise money for their initial start-up costs. In return, supporters who believed in their project are among the first to receive the proposed product, and play an important role in the start-up of the business.) This was the means by which Ethan and I would raise money for the magazine, but we weren't sure if we would actually be able to raise enough. I came across the most recently funded campaign at that time: laser-engraved, wooden food dice. The result of rolling these dice is an endless combination of dinner options. One die had your meat item, the other had your side dish. Fish + Salad. Chicken + Quinoa. Steak + Salad. The idea was simple, and yet a great success as it raised over $75,000. I told Ethan, "If people believe in a need for food dice, surely, there will be others who believe in a need for this magazine." Ethan agreed it was time to push forward with this dream. I visited a local printer, gathered together information about our future expenses, and set up a tripod to record myself awkwardly telling the world why we need a solid, Christian women's magazine.

Sometimes one of the hardest steps in pursuing a dream is simply taking the first step. This is the part where you put all your eggs in one basket and pray that it's according to God's will, preparing your heart in the instance that it's not. There were former hopes and aspirations—dreams that I sincerely thought were God's will—that turned out to be a "no" from the Lord. Photography. Germany. The list could go on. In this new venture, I knew I needed to trust God with my excitement and hold this dream loosely. Thankfully, the lessons learned in my past helped me find peace amidst uncertainty. I believed that He would bring about whatever result He deemed right and good, and that my only part to play was to listen to Him, regardless of whether my dream was a "yes" or "no" in the end.

Before launching the campaign, I put together a vision board with our magazine mission and goals. I sent it to multiple photographers, writers, and friends that I thought would also believe in the mission. To my surprise, twenty-four contributors came back and said yes to volunteering their gifts for the mission of our magazine.

To help us confirm this calling, we chose an all-or-nothing campaign. We gave ourselves thirty days to raise the needed $11,200 for our first print run. "All or nothing" means that if we raised, say, $8,000 by day thirty, all the money would be refunded and given back to the donors because we didn't meet our original goal. We chose this method because we didn't want to be tempted to pull together money we didn't have if we fell short several thousands of dollars. This was a step of faith, and we believed the result of this campaign would be the Lord's will.

To this day, I can't believe we launched knowing that we didn't have a graphic designer. A designer is vital to the layout and creation of the actual magazine. I trusted that the Lord would provide someone, and I attempted to put together my own trial copy to give future readers an idea of what we were trying to accomplish. I felt like my old college self, cramming information I didn't know just before an exam. I skimmed through an online design class that taught me how to use InDesign, and I put together a rough template of what the magazine would look like. Issue Zero was born.

It was nerve-wracking hitting "publish" on the campaign. Each one of the thirty days felt like the longest days of my life. I tried my best to not hit refresh too often, but it was hard not to follow every move. There were many moments of joy—rejoicing over complete strangers who believed in our goal. There were also moments of impatience—just simply wanting to know the outcome of whether or not we would be funded. Would this be a yes or no from God? The waiting game has never been a favorite of mine, but throughout it all, both Ethan and I remained at peace.

Freedom to Succeed

Christianity changes the way we dream. The gospel says that Jesus is king, and we are not. The gospel acknowledges that the path to true living is dying. The Bible reminds us that what is before us is passing away, and where the world esteems monetary gain and notoriety, we are wholeheartedly sold out for one mission: God's glory alone. Increasing our fame, reputation, or riches means nothing because we know that moth and rust destroy—in other words, all that stuff won't last. Our personal fame becomes futile because we know that a million likes will never amount to the love of a Father who says, "Well done." Our identity remains firmly fixed in God. We do not need the approval of men because we know that we have the righteousness of Christ. We are free from comparison because we know that God has already given us all that we need in Himself. He has given us beyond what we deserve. We know that our brothers and sisters in Christ run the same race, and we can rejoice in what God has given them here on this earth.

Success as the world knows it has lost its luster to the Christian. We leave "success" up to God and just continue to love and obey Him in the process. Because when we allow the gospel to change our views on success, then we have the freedom to be okay with whatever the outcome of our dream is. And that's the real success right there—freedom and peace. Even the most "successful" people in the world can't find those things in their dream coming true. If our dream proves to be "successful," it's to His glory. And if it doesn't prove to be "successful," it is still to His glory. This was the mind-set that kept Ethan and me at peace with the outcome of our crowd-funding campaign. We knew that He would either swing the door wide open or that He would shut it. We were free from needing the dream to come true because either way, we were successful in God's eyes because we were following Him, and we had a freedom in it all that the world can't achieve its way into.

Freedom to Fail

I posted a question on social media the other day in regard to dream-chasing: *What is one of your greatest struggles in regard to dreams, hopes, and goals?* To my surprise, one of the most common answers was fear of failure. Many of us have the head knowledge that it is God who opens and closes doors, but we all want the door-wide-open story. Some never take that first step because they are too afraid of failing.

Here is an example of what the world would consider failure: At some point when we were living in California, Ethan decided he wanted to get out of the military. In total, he applied to sixty-two different law enforcement jobs. He even flew out to Oklahoma and Maryland for interviews, both of which were not a good fit and led to closed doors. Not long after, he was offered a job from a small town in California at a sheriff's department. They were excited to hire him, and we were excited at the prospect of settling down in California. Two weeks before he dropped paperwork out of the military, they called him and told him they ran out of funding and couldn't hire him.

Sixty-two rejections. Sixty-two closed doors. Were these sixty-two failures? No, they were sixty-two *answered prayers* in response to: "Lord, may Your will be done." The living God answered us and directed our steps exactly as He saw was best! Every closed door is God directing our steps, and if we are praying that His will be done, then every closed door is an answer to prayer. God is actively working in the *nos*, in the *pauses*, in the *yeses,* and in the *not*. We need not fear the closed doors but rather be confident that He is making His will even clearer to us. A no is a step forward in discerning His will, not a step backward. Whether positive or negative, God allowed this to happen because of His infinite wisdom and divine providence. In the end, that's the Christian dreamer's secret weapon—every answer we get on a particular passion or pursuit, no matter what that answer is, is a good one that moves us forward further into God's will. As we face our own closed doors, we can ask ourselves: *How can I use this to strengthen me for the next stepping-stone?*

A Testimony of Dreams Changed

The life and legacy of Lilias Trotter (1853–1928) remains an inspiration since the moment I first read about her. Lilias was a young woman who lived in England in the late 1800s—a season where revival swept the country through key figures like D. L. Moody. Lilias was a single woman very active in Christian service. It was there she volunteered at a nearby mission, assisted in Moody's evangelistic campaigns, and taught Bible classes. She also had a great love and incredible talent for drawing and painting.

While on holiday in Italy with her mother, it just so happened that one of England's most famous painters of the Victorian era, John Ruskin, was at their same hotel. Unbeknownst to Lilias, her mom slipped some of Lilias's watercolor paintings under his doorstep with a note that asked him to review the work. Lilias had little to no formal instruction, but her mother believed in her daughter's work so much that it was worth the potential social drama that could have ensued considering their high standing in society and his own fame and repute. Ruskin loved her work; so much, in fact, that he invited her to sketch, to study other works of art, and to learn from him during their stay there. Ruskin was completely surprised by this twenty-three-year-old's giftedness and teachable spirit.

Upon returning to England she continued under his instruction while balancing her ministry in social work. After years of friendship through correspondence and occasional visits between Ruskin and Trotter, he asked Lilias to give herself wholly to developing her art. Given his status and influence, he imagined her to be a great painter whose work would be preserved and immortalized. Initially, this felt like a dream come true to Lilias. Her consideration toward this opportunity was not about fame but out of a true love for the medium. Lilias shared her thoughts on the matter in a letter to her good friend Blanche: "You will understand that it is not from vanity I tell you, at least I think not, because I know that I have no more to do with the gift than with the colour of my hair—but because I need prayer to see clearly God's way."[2] Oh, that more of us could see our natural gifts given to us as the same as our own hair or skin color—not by choice but by God's choosing.

Blanche commented on Lilias's words: "The intense delight she felt—not at the thought of fame, but at the prospect of a life given to Art and surrounded by Art—only made her seek all the more earnestly to be guided by God's Will alone."[3]

How torn Lilias must have felt. Here was one of the greatest painters of her time willing to invest his time, provide her with resources, and offer her the opportunity of a lifetime to be his apprentice at age twenty-six. After much prayer, thought, and reflection, Lilias declined Mr. Ruskin's offer. She writes: "I cannot give myself to painting in the way he means and continue still to 'seek first the Kingdom of God and His Righteousness.'"[4] In contrast to Ruskin's request of devoting herself wholly to art, Lilias wanted to devote herself wholly to something else God was asking of her, though she couldn't quite make out what exactly He was calling her to at that time. Many were surprised and saddened by her decision, and understandably so. Choosing the way of art would not have been a bad move, if that happened to be the way God was moving. But Lilias knew that in this particular case, God wasn't leading that direction.

At the age of thirty-five, God called Lilias (along with a few of her friends) to Algeria, North Africa. Algeria was completely different than the comforts of London living. Not only were she and her friends women in a foreign land, they had trouble gaining support from a mission board, so they journeyed the course with their own resources. Language proved to be a major barrier, but so did reaching the Arabic women in general whose husbands kept them sequestered in their homes. Regardless of these various challenges, Lilias stayed true to her mission, studying Arabic word-by-word, continuing to build relationships, sharing the gospel, and hosting prayer meetings as she was able. She and her two friends discovered that by reaching children, they could reach the women. Her goal was to help these women see the clear distinction between Christian salvation versus the hollow legalism of traditional Islam. Her methods of delivering this message changed from experience to experience.

One method included printing her own tracts. With the help of a translator, she and her friends hand-wrote and hand-illustrated tracts to pass out around the town. Her art proved to be useful even in this small way. Eventually, Lilias and her friends began to venture into remote villages of Algiers. These ladies endured many hardships, dangers, and continued health issues. It would have been easy to keep count of all the ways this work proved to be exhausting and discouraging. There was no way to measure results, and the result was to simply trust that seeds were sown wherever God pleased to plant them.

Lilias served in this part of the world for forty years, and the ripple effects of her life lived in obedience to God and in the power of the Holy Spirit are exponential. To this day, John Ruskin's work hangs at the Ashmolean Museum in England, along with all his other apprentices. (Some of Lilias's work is there, too, but it is filed away and only available upon request.) His work may be immortalized in an earthly sense, but Lilias's obedience led to the immortalizing of many saved souls.

Even though Lilias gave up on pursuing art as a career, she did not give up on art altogether. Throughout her journeying in North Africa, she kept journals and painted desert scenes and the groups of people she encountered, loved, witnessed to, and prayed for. God used the artistic gift He had given her to reach this part of the world in a unique way. Reproductions of her journals are available internationally, impacting lives through her drawings and words in ways that a gallery painting never could. In many ways, God did have a plan for her art to live on, but I don't think she ever imagined it would happen in this way.

Lilias went the route of obedience instead of the way of notoriety, fame, and success. It's not that pursuing a career in art is wrong in and of itself. As previously mentioned, we need Christians living as salt and light in all industries. But for Lilias, this was a matter of obedience to the calling that God placed on her life. Lilias understood this fundamental truth: God demands our obedience, and this is clearly displayed in one of her diary entries when she writes: "It is loss to keep when God says 'give.'"[5]

Lilias's life was not wasted. Her decision to forego the opportunity of a lifetime was not a failure. Though she never lived up to Ruskin's hope for her to be the greatest painter of all time, she served God with her entire being, and she listened to Him when He led her to lay down a dream for the sake of a different one.

Success Redefined

God answered our prayer in twenty-four days. Not only did He "open a door," but He allowed many to walk through it with us. Though many of our friends and family offered as they felt led, most of our support came from complete strangers. Money poured in from all over the world. $35 here, $100 there. One generous woman from California felt led to give $1,000! Another woman couldn't give but shared on her social media, and the result of her God-given platform multiplied in ways I still do not fully comprehend to this day. And there's more. Halfway through the campaign, a mutual friend named Meghan reached out about possibly designing the issue—the very thing we knew we needed most in this venture, and had been asking God to provide. After discussing the details and giving her time to pray about it, she joined our team and set out to begin working on the preliminary stages of the first issue. We set up a team of editors and our team of volunteers continued to grow. We reached our crowd-funding goal by day twenty-four, and by the end of our campaign we reached 133 percent of our goal! We went from having nothing to printing and shipping out that first issue not just to supporters here in the United States, but to readers in Singapore, Australia, and beyond.

Despite the "success" of this campaign, the reaching of our goal confirmed this as a calling—a calling that we must hold onto loosely, for He could call us away from it at any moment. To this day, our mentality remains to print issue to issue. We are not enslaved to notions that we have to grow our subscriber list or gain a bigger digital footprint in the world of social media. We walk in freedom from the pressure of business or ministry building because we have redefined Christian success. And we trust that just as God led here, He can lead us away if that is His will.

The reality is that the Christian's ultimate dream is to hear a "Well done, good and faithful servant" (Matt. 25:21, 23). Christian dreamers seek whole-heartedly after whatever it is God calls them to, whether or not God's request looks like failure or success in the world's eyes. Like Lilias, the Christian dreamer dares not hold onto the things she knows she cannot keep. She understands that it is God who holds all things together. He isn't just the sustainer of the moon, sun, and stars, but He is the sustainer of our businesses, homes, health, and every other particle of this planet. To lose our jobs, our families, our influence, or our health is devastating, but to miss the point of this life and never truly know Christ is hell.

Was Moses a failure because he never saw the promised land? Or was David a failure because he never fulfilled his dream of rebuilding the temple? There are countless examples of men and women in Scripture whose life story may not be deemed an earthly success, whose promises weren't fulfilled in their lifetime, and who had unrealized dreams. But for believers, none of these results are the point. Simply walking with God and obeying Him is.

Another important topic to consider is that failure and weakness are the means by which God's power is displayed. Allow me to be candid: *Deeply Rooted Magazine* is not a massive moneymaker. We are an ad-free publication, so we rely completely on the support of our readers, but we also print on quality paper with quality ink and quality binding. We want to support small businesses and choose to print our magazine in the United States as opposed to overseas. We believe in the importance of excellence within Christian arts and that leads to a higher production cost. I can't tell you how many times I've been told that print is dead, and that I should choose a more profitable venture, and yet God has always provided. He has always given us enough support to print issue to issue (and as I type this, we are about to print our fourteenth edition of the magazine). Our slow growth keeps me humble and dependent on the Lord, recognizing that God gives the growth. My weaknesses as a business owner and our weakness as a magazine allow us to boast in God's mighty power. Our ministry remains in existence simply because He sustains it. This is not failure nor is it success, this is His will and it's to His glory.

When we can relinquish the outcome of our dreams to God, we are free to walk confidently in pursuit of a dream as my husband and I did, or we can lay down a dream as Ms. Trotter did. Oh, that we may be Christian dreamers who are not enslaved by the fear of failure or a desire for success, but according to His will and for His glory. I may not know the dream impressed upon your heart, but I pray this freedom for you. It's the best sort of success you could ever dream of.

Chapter 8

DISCERNMENT FOR DREAMERS

"We are so busy with a million pursuits that we don't even notice the most important things slipping away."[1]

—Kevin DeYoung

I received a phone call from some Google representatives who were impressed with *Deeply Rooted* and wanted to work with us to beta test a new program. One of the questions they asked me was: "If this works the way we hope it will, are you ready to scale?" The ability to scale a business is vital. "Yes!" was my initial thought but after more pondering, I was not 100-percent sure. A business may desire growth but if it can't keep up with the demand, the result is poor customer experience and the growth they hoped for could be the death of the business. As I mentioned before, our focus has always been one issue at a time. We hadn't fully considered scaling, nor did we anticipate that our family would scale.

Two years into the business, we survived another move—this time from Fort Benning to Pennsylvania—and the birth of another sweet baby girl. In God's providence, we moved to an area where several of our *Deeply Rooted* contributors already lived, including our graphic designer and chief copy editor. And several months later when they felt called to move to China for two years, we still published several issues despite the time, distance, and poor Internet speeds. Transition, change, and rolling with the punches, so to speak, remains an ongoing occurrence for our team. As some are able to step in, others need to step out, and somehow, we manage to continue publishing magazines and, as a result, blessing the women who read it.

I often reflect on my photography days as a reminder to keep my priorities straight. I feel strongly that my first callings as a Christian woman include my relationship with God first, being a helpmate to my husband, mothering my kids, keeping our home, and serving our local church. I constantly filter my business decisions and other opportunities in light of these first callings, and the business shifts as the seasons in my life shift. After two years of quarterly issues, our team worked at a pace that we struggled to keep up with. We made the tough decision to slow down to two issues a year, and it proved to be fruitful. We had the ability to focus more on quality and not quantity.

At this point we had grown a solid online community around our brand. Not only did I want to grow this community beyond the pages of our publication and the screens on our phones, I wanted to grow it into an in-person community as well. In October of 2016, we hosted the *Deeply Rooted Retreat.* Nestled along the Appalachian Trail, more than a hundred women and myself gathered at a central Pennsylvania campground to study what it means to be deeply rooted. When we weren't attending Scripture-rich sessions, attendees tried their hand at calligraphy, wooden spoon carving, or simply enjoying nature. Between sessions we surprised the ladies with a trail mix bar and artisan donuts. The big hurrah was toward the end of our weekend when we hosted a beautiful dinner in the woods.

Globe lights strung across branches. Eucalyptus stems filled the linen-covered tables, and while everyone waited for their meal, a friend crafted espresso drinks, serving lattes and coffee in the attendees' new *Be Deeply Rooted* camp mugs. With the help of some incredible team members and friends, I put every ounce of God-given creativity I possess into this event as a means of showing these women love, offering them hospitality, and providing them a place to rest and grow deeper in their walk with God. It's nearly impossible for women to carve out time like this for their own development and rest, and it was an honor to serve them in this way.

The moments leading up to the retreat required my full focus and attention, which Ethan understood completely. We knew that the late nights, last-minute errands, and airport runs to pick up our team members were necessary. Those four days were one giant adrenaline rush. Once it was over, I was physically drained, but I discovered I also had some spiritual areas in my heart that needed attention.

The week after the retreat was very hard for me. I spent several days with so many incredible women hungry to know more about God, and the days that followed looked like me chasing down a toddler trying to convince her that changing her diaper is what's best for her. My desire to serve my family had withered in the midst of all the busyness. Motherhood didn't *feel* as important, and I knew it was time for me to reevaluate. It didn't help that I had to work ahead to release Issue 10 in time for the retreat. It didn't help that Thanksgiving and Christmas sales would soon follow the retreat. Yes, we scaled back to two issues, but I failed to look ahead and I had piled on more work for myself. We received requests for another retreat. Though my heart wanted to plan something, I knew I needed to guard my time, mind, and emotions, and to this day we still do not have immediate plans for hosting another.

The next issue after the retreat would be the last issue with the graphic designer and chief copy editor that had been with us since the beginning. In the interim, two friends stepped in and designed Issue 12 together. I headed up creative direction for the art, and once again the pace of my life drained me. Despite the fact that there was no retreat to worry about, my life still felt busy. The reality is our family was in another season of transition. We moved out of the diapers and formula stage and into the social complexities that happen at church and school. And then there were all the activities: soccer practice, soccer games, Awana, women's Bible study, the young adult's ministry Ethan led—and all the while, Ethan's schedule continued to take him away. In the midst of all this, our home had a constant shortage of clean socks and clean cups. I struggled to keep up with day-to-day tasks, and I knew another change was needed.

At the end of 2017, my team and I made the decision to scale back, yet again, to one issue per year. I was very nervous to make this change. We had already cut back once, and I wasn't sure how our subscribers would feel. The last thing I wanted for us to do is lose any momentum. When I really thought about the root of my fears, I recognized that this change went against every dream I had for myself and *Deeply Rooted,* and that it went against most business advice. I imagined us moving forward, growing, and expanding. But instead, I felt like every decision we had made over the years was backward. Much of my internal battle was because of my back and forth mindset about "success."

Despite the growing concerns in the back of my mind, both Ethan, myself, and our team had a peace about this decision. Ethan and I recorded a video explaining the change and, to our surprise, it was well received. Our sweet readers understood and respected that our family comes first, and this decision proved to be fruitful. Though our magazines are timeless, we essentially extended the shelf life by moving to an annual-issue model. This also gave us even more time to focus on quality and content. And most important, it freed me up to focus on our family life, our home, and our church commitments. In a world that says to sacrifice those right in front of you in order to grow a following of those far away from you, we chose to go the other direction.

The beauty of owning a business is that you don't have to follow the unwritten rules of this world. If my profits don't double this year, it's okay. If I don't send out those marketing e-mails this month, it's fine. If you sense the Lord leading you to cut back on production schedules or just close down altogether, then don't ignore

His promptings. I'm sure this would be deemed bad business advice, but our "success" and growth should never be at the cost of our first callings. If we are walking by the Spirit, then we must be sensitive to the Spirit's leading and not harden our hearts. We simply walk in obedience to what the Lord has called us to today—and if that means scaling back or pushing forward, we can trust Him with the end results.

Discernment for Dreamers

The discerning dreamer is willing to walk wherever the Lord calls her. So how do we know whether or not we should pursue a dream? How can we tell if we should continue with the dream we started years ago, or transition elsewhere? Anytime someone approaches me about what they should do with their dream, I always respond with the fact that there is not a one-size-fits-all answer. There is an exponential number of variants for each and every dreamer such that there is no way to address each one here. However, there are some filters that are helpful to determine whether or not someone should lay down, press pause, or move forward with a dream.

I would advise you not to read through these questions quickly. Chew on them. Mull them over in your mind. Take the time to write them out and answer them honestly. Find a quiet place and spend time praying with the Lord. Unplug from your phone and be honest with yourself.

1. What does my personal walk with God look like right now?

Taking all that I wrote in previous chapters into consideration, this question serves to be the biggest determinant of whether or not you should pursue a dream right now. I love to cook new recipes from scratch, and sometimes I have to pull out a metal sifter when baking. This handheld contraption looks like a can with a fine mesh strainer which filters any clumps that may be in the flour. Like a fine mesh sifter, this question—what my walk with God looks like right now—is intended to filter through all your passions, motives, and thoughts and cut straight to the heart.

Consider David's command to Solomon: "As for you, Solomon my son, know the God of your father, and serve him wholeheartedly and with a willing mind, for the LORD searches every heart and understands the intention of every thought. If you seek him, he will be found by you . . ." (1 Chron. 28:9). Reflect on what your personal walk with God looks like now. Do you *know* God—not just know about Him but know Him in a personal, intimate sense? Are you serving Him wholeheartedly with a willing mind? Are you seeking Him?

Now consider your spiritual walk over the course of this past week, past month, and past year. Do you have regular time dedicated to meeting with God? I know our seasons of life change faster than we'd like, which changes what our time with Him looks like, but be honest with yourself: Is the current spiritual plan you have for this particular season actually working for you? What role does Scripture play in your daily living? Are you actively praying? When it comes to pursuing a dream, having a consistent and active relationship with God is crucial. If we do not have time for the Lord now, what makes us think we will make time for the Lord in the midst of pursuing a dream? I know this is a repeated theme and should be obvious, but it bears saying: we simply will not have knowledge of God's will for our lives or sensitivity to the leading of His Spirit if we are not abiding in Him. I don't say that to condemn you or judge you. We all have our off days and experience "dry spells," so to speak. But the one who abides in Him as consistently as she can will certainly grow in knowledge, wisdom, and discernment both as she contemplates pursuing a dream and when she journeys through it.

Questions to ponder:

- Do I truly love God? Can I honestly say I long to be in His presence? Or do I have other longings that are stronger?
- Do I see a consistency in my life of time spent in the Word and in prayer? Am I eager to be in the Lord's presence? Or is it more of a dreaded "I probably should do this"? If I do not have the energy or time for personal quiet time with God, should I really consider adding something to my plate that will further steal my affection, attention, and time?
- Are my hopes, dreams, and goals sourced in an overflow of my relationship with the Lord? Do they flow from God's love and grace abounding in my own life? Or are they rooted in selfish ambition?

Many of us might get stuck here. We may know right away that our dreams take up more brain and heart space than our love for God does. We've all been in this place at some point or another, and if that is where you are at today and you feel convicted about it, praise the Lord that the Holy Spirit is working in your heart! Praise God that you don't have to remain here, that God can give you deep and abiding love for Him in the place where dread or duty used to be. Perhaps now is a good time to press pause on that dream and focus your attention on loving the Lord with all of your heart, soul, mind, and strength.

2. Does this dream line up with biblical standards for Christian living?

This may seem like a silly question to ask, but it is an important one. There may be opportunities offered to us that simply contradict the truth found in Scripture. For example, some dreams might require you to partner with organizations whose morals and ethics may conflict with God's standards. Other "dreams" may call you away from your church home for the majority of Sundays throughout the year. To protect ourselves from compromise, drifting toward worldliness, and a whole lot of future heartache, this second question helps us discern whether or not we should continue in this pursuit.

Consider this example: One of *Deeply Rooted*'s contributing photographers, Sunny Golden, shares a beautiful testimony on her website about her journey with photography and areas where she felt convicted about compromising her beliefs. Sunny lives in Hawaii, a land where beach culture is entirely different than most places. She was offered a dream assignment but upon hearing the details, questioned whether or not this was a worthy pursuit: She wrote:

> Where I live, locally designed/made brands aren't afraid to show some skin, and it's almost hard to find brands that are sensitive to modest-minded customers. I knew I didn't agree with some of the ways these companies viewed beauty, yet I was trying to figure out a way I could work with them. For weeks I found myself in the midst of a wrestling match . . . I thought up so many ideas to try to make it work, like shooting their clothing in ways that were more modest, avoiding certain angles, shooting only the items they had that covered my models the most, etc., but no matter what, each idea left me feeling like something wasn't right . . .[2]

She prayed about it, sought counsel, and after much thought and inner turmoil, declined the offer. A few weeks later another opportunity presented itself.

> It was painful to have to turn down this offer, but this time I knew that saying no was a step into the right direction. I had to trust that the Lord's conviction was a way of Him telling me this wasn't *His* best. I was tempted with success, popularity, and things that the world sees so valuable, but is that really the abundant life the Lord promises for His people? This just can't be it. I have to trust that following Him fully is well worth it; everything else is a cheap substitute. Sometimes making a decision that involves a little compromise seems like a better choice with your own human eyes. But I'm convinced that the Lord has better. I want to make a stand for what I believe in even if it means taking the rougher road and making some changes. I can trust that when the Lord puts conviction on my heart, He only wants the best for me. He has a perfect plan for my life. Will I trust the King of kings who went to die for me, or the world whose solutions lead me to dead ends and confusion?

It would have been so easy for Sunny to justify her actions and chase after her dreams in order to attain other opportunities. The devil wants us to think that these "small" compromises are not harmful, but this could not be further from the truth. Sunny is a beautiful example of someone who did not allow her dreams to blur her biblical worldview. She trusted the Lord and valued His standards above her own temporary, personal gain. And if you look up her work, you will quickly discover she has done just fine without those gigs. She doesn't have to buy into the world's standards for beauty—which often ends up in opportunities that objectify women—in order for her work to be excellent. Her work is beautiful and stands on its own, without need of the companies she rejected.

Our gauge for determining whether or not something is biblical requires an intimate knowledge of our Bibles. If biblical truth does not permeate our minds, then our own version of truth or what culture projects will have the greater influence in our decisions, and if this happens, we will head down a path of compromise.

Questions to ponder:

- Will this dream and all that is required of this dream honor the Lord? Are there any truths in Scripture that conflict with this dream? What are they?
- If I do sense some sort of compromise, am I making justifications in my mind about why pursuing this dream is okay?

3. What are my motives for pursuing this dream?

While the dream we chase after may not be morally wrong, we can still have wrong motives. We must trace the root of what is driving us. We may seek the applause of a crowd or the approval of a loved one. Galatians 1:10 says, ". . . If I were still trying to please people, I would not be a servant of Christ." Paul understood that pleasing men is directly opposed to pleasing God. If we are pursuing a dream with any bent on building a name for ourselves and seeking approval of others, then this may be a good time to reevaluate our dream before moving further along in the process. A true biblical pursuit does not require the affirmation of others; rather, it is obedience to what the Lord may be calling you to do.

Questions to ponder:

- Why do I feel led to pursue this dream? Are my motives rooted in biblical ideas like spreading the good news of the gospel, being a light in this specific industry, sharing a gift God gave me

> to edify others, enjoying a way God wired me, providing for my family, and giving Him glory for it? Or am I doing this to be seen, known, or loved? Is my longing for this dream flowing from a heart that desires purpose, power, wealth, worth, or fame?

4. What season of life am I in right now?

Life is a journey and it is filled with a variety of stages, phases, and seasons. The life of a single woman in college looks totally different than the woman with young kids, and both of those lifestyles look different from the retired widow. Though our callings in Christ remain the same, our responsibilities and schedules vary. Regardless of what season we are in, Scripture gives clear calls for the woman. Titus 2 says:

> Older men are to be self-controlled, worthy of respect, sensible, and sound in faith, love, and endurance. In the same way, older women are to be reverent in behavior, not slanderers, not slaves to excessive drinking. They are to teach what is good, so that they may encourage the young women to love their husbands and to love their children, to be self-controlled, pure, workers at home, kind, and in submission to their husbands, so that God's word will not be slandered. (vv. 2–5)

Just as men are commanded to exhibit self-control, respectability, sensibility, soundness of faith, love, and endurance, women are too. Women are also called to be respectful and sober, ones who build another up instead of slandering or tearing someone down. Though this is addressed to the older women, the model that Titus gives is for the older to teach the younger; therefore, the young woman should aspire to bear these qualities as well. Continuing on, the older women are supposed to help the younger ones learn what is good, as well as learn how to engage in their homes, which for many includes loving their husbands, kids, and so forth. (For single women this would mean honoring and loving parents or roommates and brothers and sisters in Christ, which are our ultimate family in the Lord.) These are all first callings. God saw fit to include this portion in Scripture and, despite culture's ever-changing definition of womanhood and femininity, we must seek to honor God's timeless Word in this way of living.

I am not here to argue whether or not a woman should work outside of the home. There are those who land on one side, saying that "workers at home" means just that—the home and the home alone should be the work sphere of the woman. There are others who land on the other side, saying that "workers at home" points to domestic needs as well as a vocational "job." They might argue that the domestic and the economic spheres overlapped in ancient times. Both sides of the argument pull from different passages of Scripture. Some point to Lydia and the Proverbs 31 woman who sold her goods at the city gate, noting that women were an ancient version of small business owners. Others point to all the mother-heroes throughout the Scriptures, noting that glory and wonder of motherhood and homemaking that the world has deemed "not good enough."

More than sharing my own opinions on the matter, I long for each of you to be "fully convinced in his own mind" (Rom. 14:5), and I wholeheartedly believe that as you grow in the knowledge of Jesus you will have all wisdom and discernment through the power of the Holy Spirit to navigate that question in your own church, family, and home.

The bottom line is that we see a priority here in Scripture and it does not point to a high-profile successful life as the world would define, but instead, points to loving those right in front of you—in your very home and neighborhood. This is how we love God and love our closest neighbors (our husbands, parents, roommates, neighbors, and children). This is how we honor God's Word so that people do not slander Him.

We also must remember that Titus 2 is a letter written from Paul to Titus, and its purpose was to help him pastor a *church.* Paul's instruction here is not given to individuals, necessarily, but is all in the context of the larger, local church congregation. This, along with passages like Hebrews 10:24–25, which tells us not to neglect meeting together as a body, help us see that included within our list of first callings is active involvement in a local church. In an age where commitment is not taken seriously, have we committed ourselves to church membership? We know that church membership does not save us or earn us extra Jesus points, but it does express our devotion to the local body God has called us to. It reveals that we make much of the spouse that Jesus makes much of—His bride. Church membership offers its members accountability, and it testifies to our support of church leadership and willingness to be shepherded underneath their leadership. Are we serving in our local church? Chapter 7 touched on how our spiritual gifts and natural abilities were given to us for the building up of the Church body. Consider the current needs of your local church—not just monetarily, but in acts of service. Are there shortages in the church nursery? Can you give of your time for women's discipleship, for prayer nights, for the worship ministry, for Wednesday night children's programs?

Lastly, passages like Proverbs 4:26 tell us to carefully consider the paths our feet are walking down—to look ahead to where we are headed. Here, a final question we can ask is: "What future seasons are before me?" We obviously cannot know everything that lies ahead in life, but if you have a dream that you want to pursue and are pregnant with your first child, for example, is now a good time to start? You may have the time now to move forward but when your baby arrives, will you have the energy to multitask? Have you considered the early stages of their life or what your family plan looks like? When I started *Deeply Rooted,* I had Kaiden who was around two and a half and Skye who was maybe four months. I was in an easy season where Kaiden had a solid afternoon nap, Skye had multiple naps, and they were both in bed by 7:00 p.m. Ethan worked late nights so their bedtime equaled Mommy's work time. A little over a year later, we moved to Pennsylvania, Skye entered a more mobile phase, and I was pregnant with our third. Life was so much busier, and we didn't have a solid routine. But when Ethan deployed, once again I had every night to work by myself. When he came back, was adapted our schedule once more.

Kids or no kids, every season in a woman's life is different, and comes with another set of commitments, needs, requirements, and capacity. Every season calls for yet another evaluation, depending on what's coming down the pike. For me, that meant another child, or a different age for a current child. For you, the next seasons of life might hold taking care of a sick parent, finishing another semester of school, getting married, ministering in a new capacity at church, or helping a neighbor for an extended season with a particular need God is calling you to meet. All of our specifics will look different, but we can all consider the future season ahead of us as we consider pursuing our dream. And take heart that we all have something else—something more important—in common as well. As Christians, we all have the same first callings, fixed pursuits that never change.

Questions to ponder:

- What callings in Titus 2 apply to me right now?
- *For those who are married:* Do I love my husband? Do I make loving, supporting, respecting him, and meeting his needs a priority in my life? This may be very hard to hear and do, but sometimes the best person to answer this question is him. We give and receive love differently, and sometimes we can be blind to our own habits. The last thing we want is for the dream we are

pursuing to become a source of resentment for our spouses. Even if your husband does not play an active role in chasing your dream, he will play a supporting role as we all know that dreams require blood, sweat, tears, and a whole lot of encouragement for the harder days.

- *For those with kids:* Do I value the gift of motherhood? It's so easy to view our roles as moms as unfulfilling, purposeless, or "in the way" of what we really want to do. Not only is this a lie from the devil, but this belief shapes our attitude and actions when a child knocks over his cup for the third time this week or when he forgot his homework at school once again. If we lack contentment in motherhood now, we will surely not find it there when we pursue our dream. Our kids know what it is that we love and if we prioritize a dream above them, they will notice too.
- Have I considered membership at my church? In what ways do I give of my time, money, and resources?
- What might next year look like? Or five years from now look like? How does this square with the dream I have? Could these things work in tandem with it? Can I still maintain my first callings? Of course, we are never 100-percent certain about our future. James 4:13–14 reminds us not to boast about tomorrow because we have absolutely no idea what it will bring, and this is why we are told to add the disclaimer to our plans, "according to His will." However, considering these questions will help us consider the

various life seasons and changes that may come our way in the coming years.

5. Have I sought counsel in this?

"A fool's way is right in his own eyes, but whoever listens to counsel is wise" (Prov. 12:15). Sometimes an idea may sound great in our head but when we actually vocalize it to other people, things can change. Before I launched *Deeply Rooted*, I consulted my husband, parents, in-laws, pastor, and trusted business friends. It was important to know that I had a solid support system not only advising me but also praying for me. There were other complexities to consider in regard to magazine-making, and the Lord graciously provided two women already in the magazine industry to help answer any logistical questions I had. We need iron-sharpens-iron type of people in our life to help us untangle the various affections of our heart and to offer another perspective.

Questions to ponder:

- What does my spouse, mentor, parent, pastor, or best friend say about this? How does their input line up with my thoughts on the matter? Have we prayed about this together?
- Have I talked to other trusted industry professionals about my idea for this dream?
- And if I'm not currently seeking counsel, why not? What is my biggest fear in seeking the input and advice of others?

6. What logistics are required to make this dream happen?

My temptation when I am offered an incredible opportunity is to say yes right away, but there are many factors involved in any pursuit. If our dream is to launch a new business or nonprofit, market research is important. Is there a product out there that meets this need already?

If so, how will yours be better? Another consideration is that start-up costs can be a major factor. Will you need a dedicated work space? Do you need to front money for inventory? Have you considered the costly applications for business permits and applications, patents, and trademarks?

For the magazine, I had to consider what up-front expenses there were. This included everything from website hosting to the product itself. I had to consider what shipping materials were required, shipping costs, and what software we needed to manage our shipping.

Time is another factor to consider. Though working stay-at-home moms are home all day, they have brief windows where they can actually be alone, and those windows are very inconsistent and change from season to season. Shipping a physical magazine meant wrapping and packaging orders. Thankfully, as we launched issues, I had the help of friends but, overall, I was the one primarily packaging product for the first four years. This was time-consuming and it took me away from my family. There were nights when Ethan and I spent our evening packaging together. (However, we did make it fun and would watch a movie while wrapping magazines or we would just catch up on our days.) We made sacrifices in order to save money in our early stages.

For you, the logistics involved will obviously look different for your dream. But considering those logistics is nonnegotiable. You have to consider them, because they will be the stuff of "chasing that dream" in future years.

Questions to ponder:

- Am I filling a need or does something like this already exist? Do some market research and see if there is already another business or ministry you can join efforts with.
- How much time and effort will this take? Based on my current schedule, I will need to determine

what pockets of time I have available to focus on this dream. Am I able to commit to sticking to this schedule? Consider what goals or milestones I would like to achieve and when I hope for those things to happen.

- Will I need assistance? Am I doing this on my own or will I have a team of people to help me? Will those people be volunteers? If not, how will I pay them?
- Can I afford this venture? What methods of funding have I considered?
- What legalities should I consider? Are there copyright laws I need to look into? Patents? Client contracts? Trademark? What about business licenses, re-sellers permits, or liability coverage?
- Am I relying on this for income? How does this fare with my means of income now?

These questions aren't meant to make you feel defeated or quench your bright fire, but to prepare you as best as possible as you consider a passion you have. Consider Acts 6:1–7, which parses out logistics in regard to who is going to preach and who is going to serve the widows overlooked in the daily distribution of the early church. Even when it comes to the earliest stages of Christianity, the people who fared the best with a dream have thought these things through, and you would be doing yourself a disservice not to do likewise.

7. Am I willing to surrender this dream to God?

I wholeheartedly believe that before we can ever move forward with a dream, we must first be willing to surrender it to God. In holding our dreams and plans for ourselves loosely, we posture ourselves as Mary surrendered her will to the Lord in bearing Christ, "'I am the Lord's servant,' said Mary. 'May it be done to me according to your word'" (Luke 1:38). We must lay our dreams down before we ever pick them up, for if we hold to this dream tightly now, we will continue to keep a tight grip on it as it grows.

Questions to ponder:

- Have I surrendered this idea to God?
- Am I okay with life apart from this dream? Will I be content if God doesn't allow this dream to come to fruition?
- If God does allow this dream to come true, can I walk away from it if He ever calls me away from it?

My prayer is that these questions give you framework to filter through whether or not you should pursue, press pause, or lay down the dream stirring in your heart. If you were stuck at some point on any of these questions, and don't feel that you can answer them confidently, that is okay. Just because you press pause or lay down a dream now does not mean He cannot resurrect it later. And even if you pursue one now in good confidence and find that it isn't the perfect fit you thought it would be, God can help you course-correct even then, as He did with me and my photography experience.

If these questions helped affirm the dream stirring within, then wonderful! I am so glad you are at peace with what you believe the Lord is leading you to. Regardless of whatever conclusion or lack of conclusion you have come to, "seek first the kingdom of God and his righteousness, and all these things will be provided for you" (Matt. 6:33).

Truth be told, these questions don't end even if you do pursue the dream. I still use these questions to filter all our future decisions, and they continue as a guide in our magazine endeavors. Every step of the way for us has felt so counterintuitive to how a business should be run, but we are confident that we are walking in obedience to God.

Though some of these decisions have been difficult, the knowledge that this has been God's operation from the start has allowed us to hold *Deeply Rooted* both excitedly and loosely at the same time. The Lord may do with it as He pleases, and I know that even the seasons that called for "backward steps" were really a step forward in my walk with Him.

Chapter 9

GOD'S WILL FOR THE CHRISTIAN DREAMER

"Your kingdom come. Your will be done on earth as it is in heaven."

—MATTHEW 6:10

By 2018, the military tasked Ethan with another deployment. Our family prepared for the inevitable, but we never anticipated the destination: Germany! God had written Europe into our story once more. My husband spent several months overseas, and my son and I had the opportunity to live with him for almost a whole month while my mom cared for our girls. My European dream came true after all, and I cannot help but smile when I remember the Dianne from many years before crying in frustration over the loss of our Germany assignment.

I am also amazed when I look back and think about my hesitancy to transition to *Deeply Rooted*'s single, annual issue. I moved forward with the decision in peace having considered the ways I had seen Him work in our past, but that still did not negate the real feelings of disappointment in changing our production schedule. Again, God had a plan. As I continued seeking God's will, not just for *Deeply Rooted* but for our family, we felt strongly about committing to a year of homeschooling. Just as I never anticipated being a stay-at-home mom, I never imagined myself as a homeschooling mom. Here was another decision that, from a cultural standpoint, didn't make sense.

At this point in our time line, Kaiden was already in school full-time, Skye would be full-time as well in the next school year, and Cora would enter preschool a few times a week. There would be *actual days* where I could have dedicated to myself! I could spend all that time working on home needs plus *Deeply Rooted,* and it would give me more margin to pursue everything on my to-do list because all the kids would be out of the house for a solid several hours.

Why in the world would I choose homeschooling when "freedom" was just around the corner? I battled loving and valuing the role of motherhood since that April Fool's Day when I found out I would become a parent. But over the course of the eight years of Kaiden's life, God softened my heart and gave me eyes to see the very real kingdom work that motherhood is. And pouring into my family the way I could through homeschooling made sense for us at the time—well, heavenly sense anyway. I knew God called us to this lifestyle change for this one year, and that meant joyfully prioritizing the needs of my family over my personal ambitions. Now, this is not to say that mothers who send their kids off to public or private school are wrong. We have tried all of the above and understand that each has its pros and cons. Every family has to make the decision that lines up with God's specific leading in their specific home. But for us, we knew He was asking us to do this for our own various reasons. And here's the thing: we wouldn't have been able to homeschool had *Deeply Rooted* not cut down to one issue. Scaling back needed to happen to prepare for this family transition. To further confirm God's hand in this, Ethan ended up taking a new position that would call him away even more frequently, but with homeschooling, we could travel alongside him. This way, the kids would get time with their dad. And military families especially know just how precious that is. Once again, God knew.

He had more written for our story even still. One month before our Summer 2018 Issue 13 release, I received an e-mail from an editor at B&H Publishing. I was not sure what would come of the e-mail, but was eager to hear what she had to say. "We love what *Deeply*

Rooted is doing and typically when there is a great ministry like this, there is usually someone behind it that has a story to share." We talked about the creation of *Deeply Rooted* and how God worked through it from the beginning. Our conversation ended with the editor asking me to submit a book proposal. I could hardly believe what I heard! There I was, going through those very same questions I mentioned in the last chapter to help me wisely evaluate what my final response should be, in spite of what my emotional response was in the moment. I examined my heart. I thought about where I was spiritually. I considered how our family and home life had been. Ethan and I prayed about it. We sought counsel. I evaluated what it would look like with my current schedule. So many filters ran through my brain. I truly and honestly felt so unworthy for the task, but my sweet husband was an incredible encouragement to me at this time. Ethan and I decided that I should submit a proposal and that the response of the publishing team would determine whether or not we move forward. We asked God to slam the door shut if this was not His will. He did it many times before and could very well do it again.

Several months passed and I finally heard a response: a book deal was in the works! I did nothing to pursue this opportunity and yet God laid it out so clearly before me. If I could go back in time and tell the seven-year-old Dianne who wanted to be a cashier, the eighteen-year-old Dianne who wanted to be an English teacher, and the twenty-year-old Dianne who wanted to be a professional photographer that one day I would find joy, contentment, and hope in God's unfailing love, that I would be the wife to an incredible husband, a mother and teacher to three amazing kids, and that one day I would own a magazine and write a book, I doubt I would believe myself. The story God has written for me is far better than any I could ever write for myself—but not because of marriage or motherhood and not because making a magazine seems fun or writing a book sounds glamorous. No, even these things are laborious and difficult. The real "win" in my story is that I found out true joy *really is* found in the Lord alone, and it is the result of being in His will—which takes discernment and obedience, no matter how unfair or strange His will seems like in the moment. God has used both hardship and opportunity to draw me closer to Him, and it is here I've discovered that He is all-satisfying, no matter what He calls me to. There is absolutely nothing I could have done in my own strength or ability to make any of this happen on my own. Every portion of my story has clearly been the Lord directing my path. He has laid out stepping-stone after stepping-stone, and by His grace and in the power of the Holy Spirit I've had the faith to take step after step. The reality is that God's will has prevailed throughout my lifetime, and His will will prevail through yours too as you seek Him first.

Maybe you are at the end of this book and you still don't have a 100-percent for-sure answer of what to do. I wish I knew your life story and your passions and your hopes and dreams. I wish we could sit and have coffee and you could share with me how you came to know Jesus and how you believe He is leading you today. But even if this were possible, and even if we were the closest of friends, I would tell you that I don't have all of the answers, that none of us do. We are finite, limited beings and that reality frustrates us.

Consider that there is nothing that God does that is without purpose. This includes His intentionally leaving out the specific details in the blueprint that is your life. He wants you to turn to Him, depend on Him, press into Him, and seek Him. And where He hasn't provided step-by-step directions for specific situations, He *has* laid out His overarching will for all believers in Scripture. In the first chapter of Ephesians, the Christian is told that God has chosen us to be holy and blameless, adopted through Jesus who gave us redemption by His blood and forgiveness of our trespasses. He has clearly laid out our path and the end goal of that path is "to bring everything together in Christ, both things in heaven and things on earth in him" (Eph. 1:10).

We also are told that His will for us is:

- to repent and believe in Him. (Mark 1:15)
- to love Him with our entire being. (Mark 12:30)
- to love our neighbors. (Mark 12:31)
- to be sanctified, to remain pure, and grow in holiness. (1 Thess. 4:3–7)
- to do good works. (1 Peter 2:15)
- to live in a spirit of gratitude, be constant in prayer, and be joyfully content. (1 Thess. 5:16–18)

This and so much more is found within the pages of Scripture, and every time you feel frustrated that your stepping-stones may not seem clear, turn to His Word to see the bigger picture and keep trusting Him. Remember that if you are fighting for these things above, *you are walking in His will.*

Walk by Faith

Shortly after I married Ethan, I attended a special military spouse's day when a massive event hall was filled with tables where vendors offered free goodies at every turn. There were complimentary boxes of Girl Scout Cookies, stations for paraffin hand wax treatments, and toward the front of the room several massage therapists offered free five-minute massages. I made my way across the venue and sat down for my massage. As my face pressed into the awkward foam chair, I wondered who else's face was there before mine, but the moment the masseuse's hands touched my shoulders I didn't seem to care anymore. The next five minutes were pure bliss. She hit every tight area of my neck and the relief felt heavenly—until I stood up.

As I opened my eyes, my vision blurred and all I could see was darkness. Go figure, Ethan was nowhere near me and I began to panic. Nothing like this had ever happened to me before and I was not sure what to do. I maneuvered myself around tables and random bodies, until I finally made my way to my husband. Praise the Lord, it was then that my sight slowly came back.

Apparently, a mixture of dehydration and the pressure of my face pressed into the chair rest caused some sort of temporary vision loss. Though I have no desire to go back to that experience, God used those visionless moments to remind me what it means to not walk by sight. Walking by faith instead of sight is not easy. We don't like that we can't see what's ahead. We don't like that we aren't in control. But this is faith, and the walking part (it's movement, it's action) is living out that faith. This is why we must: "Trust in the Lord with all your heart, and do not rely on your own understanding; in all your ways know him, and he will make your paths straight" (Prov. 3:5–6). He will lay out our path and we have the privilege of watching it unfold one step at a time. As we live out that list above by the power of the Holy Spirit, our hearts and minds are transformed and renewed and it is then that we are able to "discern what is the good, pleasing, and perfect will of God" (Rom. 12:2).

Dreaming requires walking by faith. We forego what is seen to trust in the unseen. I can look back at my own story and see that so many steps did not make sense from a worldly point of view, but we knew God was still at work, and so we obeyed anyway. Maybe God will call you backward when you *really, really, really* want to move forward with a dream. Maybe He will call you to move forward when you *really, really, really* don't feel ready or capable. Either way, don't walk by sight. Walk by faith that God knows what He's doing.

Don't Waste Your Life

I'm going to go there with you right now. I'm going to lay the truth on thick, and I'm not going to apologize for it. Too many Christian books on reaching your goals and dreams and potential don't mention these things, yet these truths are all that will matter in the end. If I didn't mention them, I wouldn't actually love you as a sister (or brother) in the Lord. Ready? Here we go.

It is all too easy to get caught up in pursuing our dreams, perfecting our craft, and making a name for ourselves here on earth. But remember: any sinful desires for fame or fortune will one day reveal themselves to be worthless. In fact, they will be worse than worthless. The "hope and future" they promise result in death if they lead you on the road to destruction and cause you to miss out on the narrow gate (Matt. 7:13–14). One day every knee will bow and every tongue will confess the point of our entire existence: Jesus is Lord. The verdict for each life will either be, "Well done, good and faithful servant!" or, "I never knew you. Depart from me, you lawbreakers" (Matt. 25:21, 23; 7:23). This reality should sober every single one of us, and cause us to "Test yourselves to see if you are in the faith. Examine yourselves. Or do you yourselves not recognize that Jesus Christ is in you?—unless you fail the test" (2 Cor. 13:5). Are we hearers of the Word only, or are we doers too (James 1:23–25)? These are the things that will be asked of us in the end.

It is for this reason that we throw off the cultural chains that we once so happily put on ourselves. Where we once thought that the pursuit of our dreams would bring ultimate happiness, purpose, and fulfillment, we now find that purpose in God alone. Though pursuing a dream may well be God's will for us in this season of our lives (or may well not be), we no longer succumb to the lie that our hope rests in that dream's fulfillment. We have put off the old self along with the old ways, to put on the new. We must live no longer corrupted by "deceitful desires" but rather "renewed in the spirit of your minds" (Eph. 4:22–23).

We understand that prioritizing the pursuit of dreams is a life-or-death matter. We know that we came into this world with nothing and we will take nothing out of it. As we give our account to Christ, we will be laid bare: "stripped of any façade of respectability, and openly revealed in the full and true reality of one's character."[1] We know that God sees not as man sees, where man looks at the outward appearance, God looks at the heart (1 Sam. 16:7). First Corinthians 3:11–15 says:

> For no one can lay any other foundation than what has been laid down. That foundation is Jesus Christ. If anyone builds on the foundation with gold, silver, costly stones, wood, hay, or straw, each one's work will become obvious. For the day will disclose it, because it will be revealed by fire; the fire will test the quality of each one's work. If anyone's work that he has built survives, he will receive a reward. If anyone's work is burned up, he will experience loss, but he himself will be saved—but only as through fire.

As we stand before Jesus, we will not have a phone in hand, saying, "See, look at how many social media followers I have." We will also not have our bank statements laid before Him saying, "Look at how much money I accumulated in my lifetime." He won't be impressed with our toys or our platform or our perfectly curated life. He won't find our excuses understandable and He won't find our deflective attempts at humor endearing.

Whatever we do, sisters, may it all be to the glory of God because if it's not, it burns up. It misses the point. And God knows. He knows when everything you do is done for the wrong reason. He knows when you want some sort of big break for the sake of your own kingdom or fame or renown instead desiring it out of joyfulness for the gift He gave you and as a means to glorify Him and build up others.

Scripture is clear that Christians will give an account of their lives: "For we must all appear before the judgment seat of Christ, so that each may be repaid for what he has done in the body, whether good or evil" (2 Cor. 5:10). While the Christian will not be judged for sin here (since our sin was already judged at the cross), we will receive a reward for the works done truly to glorify God and not out of selfish ambition. Some questions we can ask ourselves are: Am I a fruitful Christian? Have I stood the test so that I may "receive the crown of life that God has promised to those who love him" (James 1:12)? Peter describes what this looks like when he writes in 2 Peter 1:5–10:

> For this very reason, make every effort to supplement your faith with goodness, goodness with knowledge, knowledge with self-control, self-control with endurance, endurance with godliness, godliness with brotherly affection, and brotherly affection with love. For if you possess these qualities in increasing measure, they will keep you from being useless or unfruitful in the knowledge of our Lord Jesus Christ. The person who lacks these things is blind and shortsighted and has forgotten the cleansing from his past sins. Therefore, brothers and sisters, make every effort to confirm your calling and election, because if you do these things you will never stumble.

Let us not be shortsighted Christians that chase after worldly pleasures and pursuits, forgetting what it is that we are saved from and Whom we should live for. While God may call us to pursue something that He planted in our heart for His kingdom purposes, we must check our impulses often. Yes, He made us unique. Yes, He gave us gifts. Yes, He wants us to fan those things into flame. But we can easily make all those things about building our own empire and becoming a big deal in the world's eyes. And let me tell you: going that route, even with something God may legitimately be calling you toward, will make you miserable.

Solomon is a perfect example. God laid out His desired plans for Solomon. But Solomon's heart got compromised in the process, tangled up in fame and power and lust, and he didn't finish strong. God led him a direction and handed him a dream, and Solomon mishandled it all in the end. We must remember our fallen nature in the midst of dream-chasing—even if we get a "yes" from God, we must tread carefully and keep our hearts in check. If we don't, dream-chasing will make you miserable in this life, and worse than that, it won't go over well on the Last Day before the Lord. I know all this sounds harsh and it's not wrapped in the typical flowery language we see about dreaming on social media, but it's the truth. And I care about dreamers too much not to tell them this part of the deal when it comes to ambition, pursuit, and passions.

Future Glory

There will be no copies of *Deeply Rooted Magazine* in heaven. There will be no copies of this book either. The dreams you have for yourself, no matter how great the aspiration, will fade away. All these things are passing. I don't mean to belittle the desires planted within our hearts. It's not that our dreams don't matter—they do—but the pursuits of this life, valuable as they may be presently, are a means to an end; the end being Jesus crowned Lord of all! Yes, it's a noble pursuit to build wells in Africa, but we build the wells not just to satisfy a temporary need (though that's massively important!) but as a means of offering the living water. Yes, we have the Christian freedom to start a blog or grow our Etsy shop, but the end goal is to glorify God in doing so.

Piper writes, ". . . any good-hearted goal, without the desire to give people eternal joy in God, is condemnation with a kind face. Love always wants what is best for the needy and what's best is enjoying God fully and forever."[2] We should boldly proclaim the gospel through the big and small platforms that God has given to each one of us. The career, the product, whatever the result of your dream may be will fade; however, the fruit of gospel advancement from these things will have eternal ramifications. The souls saved by the life-changing work of the gospel through your work is what bears fruit, makes disciples, and offers a life-changing, life-transforming eternal difference. And this is where I get excited. Yes, *Deeply Rooted Magazine* may not be in heaven, but the Christian women who were built up by it will be.

The gospel changes absolutely everything about our dreaming! Because of Jesus and His calling on our lives, we have the freedom to move forward with, press pause on, or lay down our dreams. Our boast is no longer in ourselves or our accomplishments but is in Him alone. The gospel transforms us from being me-centered to He-centered. Do you see it? He is the end goal. He is the pursuit of all pursuits. He is the dream! Knowing, loving, and serving Him is the greatest accomplishment we can ever achieve. An eternity with God is the prize! And as we walk in a manner worthy of Him, as we seek His will for our lives, in return, He offers us a peace that passes all understanding and eternal joy.

Sweet sister in Christ, when Jesus becomes our absolute delight, we are free to follow wherever He calls us. Whether you choose to move forward with your dream, press pause on it, or lay it at the foot of the cross, as a Christian you have every ability to live a life of peace, contentment, and gratitude knowing that your life does have purpose. You are not "filler," but rather play a significant role in God's plan for eternity, whether that be in the particular dream you have right now, or in some other way He may lead you. He has entrusted you with spiritual gifts and those gifts contribute to the Church that awaits the coming of the Bridegroom. Though your efforts and energies may not be seen by the world, He sees.

The Christian dreamer is secure knowing her identity is anchored in the Eternal One, not in something that quickly fades. In a world of girl-bosses, championing other women around them only to build their own kingdoms, we need more women laying down their lives for the sake of the gospel and boldly following the Lord no matter what He calls them to. While there's nothing wrong with owning a business or working hard, we need women who are doing so marked by the fruit of the Spirit—women who embody peace, patience, and self-control rather than restlessness, discontent, rivalry, and ingratitude. My heart longs to see women using their God-given gifts in their local churches, building up the body with all zeal, fervor, and passion. Oh, the freedom to be found when we lay our dreams at the foot of the cross and trust that God can resurrect and use our desires in His perfect timing according to His will! May we come to recognize that His eternal plan of salvation for lost souls is greater than our fleeting desires for self-exaltation. May this mission be one of the major focuses of our life's ministry. May we proclaim the words of Paul: "My eager expectation and hope is that I will not be ashamed about anything, but that now as always, with all courage, Christ will be highly honored in my body, whether by life or by death. For me, to live is Christ and to die is gain" (Phil. 1:20–21). And the best part is that if we are these kinds of women, obedience will always result in peace, regardless of how the world measures our successes or lack thereof. The real win for us will be that whether we succeed or fail by the world's standards, *we won't care so much.*

I heard this in a sermon once, and it stuck with me: "It's not perfect performance of the will of God, but persistent purposing to do it."[3] God does not expect perfection in this lifetime—that is what Christ has imputed to us. We will fail. We will mess up. We didn't earn our salvation by our merits and we don't maintain it by our merit, but we do keep moving forward in cooperation with Him as He changes us to be more like His Son. When the world's lies tempt us to move off course and when we fall prey to the devil's schemes, may we pick ourselves back up again, confess our sin, and press on. As we immerse ourselves in Scripture, pray without ceasing, participate in the church body, serve one another, love our families, keep our homes, may we ask God for steadfastness, endurance, and strength to keep running our individual races. May we not grow weary in doing good (Gal. 6:9); rather, may we be "steadfast, immovable, always excelling in the Lord's work" (1 Cor. 15:58). Let's "fight the good fight" (1 Tim. 6:12) alongside one another—even as we consider our dreams—in all love, patience, and humility.

We do not live for this kingdom. "For we do not have an enduring city here; instead, we seek the one to come" (Heb. 13:14). The future glory we await—the resurrection—is beyond our wildest dreams. We know that one day we will encounter the new heaven and earth where there is no more death, pain, hurts, or tears. Comparison and envy will be destroyed. Any desires for self-gain, obliterated. True joy, happiness, and blessedness will satisfy us eternally as we worship and walk in the presence of the King of kings—the One who walked with us through our ordinary days, our hard days, our best days, and our dreaming days too. Until that day, I urge you with this: "live worthy of the calling you have received, with all humility and gentleness, with patience, bearing with one another in love, making every effort to keep the unity of the Spirit through the bond of peace" (Eph. 4:1–3). As God moves you to lay down a dream, press pause on a dream, or pursue a dream, always remember how trustworthy He is in whatever He asks you to do. Stay faithful in the first callings, listen to Him when He's leading forward or backward with a certain hope you have, and trust Him with all the rest—when you do, you'll be the freest dreamer the world has ever seen, glorifying Him and walking worthy of all He has called you to.

NOTES

Chapter 1

1. Iain Duguid, *Living in the Gap Between Promise and Reality* (P&R Publishing, 1999), 36.

2. Thomas Watson, *The Ten Commandments* (West Linn, OR: Christian Publication Resource Foundation, n.d.).

3. Robert Robinson, "Come Thou Fount" (1757).

4. John Piper, "He Will Send His Angels Before You," Sermon, Bethlehem Baptist Church, Minneapolis, MN, August 8, 1982.

5. Robert Robinson, "Come Thou Fount" (1757).

Chapter 2

1. Gregory K. Beale, *We Become What We Worship: A Biblical Theology of Idolatry* (Downers Grove, IL: IVP Academic, 2008), 49.

2. Charles Haddon Spurgeon, "Prayer, the Proof of Godliness," Sermon, The Metropolitan Tabernacle Pulpit, Newington, October 27, 1887.

3. Beale, *We Become What We Worship*, 307.

4. John Piper, *God Is the Gospel* (Wheaton, IL: Crossway, 2005), 15.

5. Wayne Grudem, *Systematic Theology* (Grand Rapids, MI: Zondervan, 1994), 657.

6. John Woodhouse (ed. Kent Hughes), *1 Samuel: Looking for a Leader* (Preaching the Word Series) (Crossway, Nov. 2014), 41–45.

7. Charles Spurgeon, *The Spurgeon Study Bible* (Nashville, TN: Holman Bible Publishers, 2017), 1575.

Chapter 3

1. I. Lilias Trotter, *Parables of the Cross* (Oxvision Books, 2015), 32.

2. Merrill C. Tenney, *Zondervan Pictorial Bible Dictionary* (Grand Rapids, MI: Zondervan, 1967), 647.

3. These were rules established by God given to His people for the proper "form" of worship and rules for how they were to conduct themselves when offering prayers or sacrifices to God.

4. J. I. Packer, *Concise Theology: A Guide to Historic Christian Beliefs* (Carol Stream, IL: 2001), 82–83.

Chapter 4

1. R. C. Sproul, "The Bible Story," Ligonier Ministries, September 1, 2015, https://www.ligonier.org/learn/articles/bible-story/.

2. For books on how to study Scripture, see *Living By the Book: The Art and Science of Reading the Bible* by Howard G. Hendricks and William D. Hendricks, *How to Study Your Bible: Discover the Life-Changing Approach to God's Word by* Kay Arthur, David Arthur, and Pete De Lacy*; How to Read the Bible Book by Book* by Gordon Fee and Douglass Stuart; *Grasping God's Word: A Hands-On Approach to Reading, Interpreting, and Applying the Bible* by J. Scott Duvall and J. Daniel Hays; and *Women of the Word: How to Study the Bible with Both Our Hearts and Our Minds* by Jen Wilkin.

Chapter 6

1. Quote written specifically for author.

2. Michael Horton, *Ordinary* (Grand Rapids, MI: Zondervan, 2014), 16.

3. Kevin DeYoung, "Stop the Revolution. Join the Plodders," Ligonier Ministries, 9 Sept. 2016, www.ligonier.org/blog/stop-the-revolution-join-the-plodders/. Also see Eugene Peterson's *A Long Obedience in the Same Direction* (Downers Grove, IL: IVP, 2000).

Chapter 7

1. Isabella Trotter, *First Impressions of the New World* (London, Longman, 1859), vi.

2. Blanche A. F. Pigott, *I. Lilias Trotter: Founder of the Algier Mission Band* (London: Marshall, Morgan & Scott, 1929), 11.

3. Ibid.

4. Ibid.

5. I. Lilias Trotter, *Parables of the Cross* (Urbana, IL: Project Gutenberg, n.d.).

Chapter 8

1. Kevin DeYoung, *Crazy Busy* (Wheaton, IL: Crossway, 2013), 23.
2. Sunny Golden, "Staying True to Your Convictions," April 3, 2016.

Chapter 9

1. Paul Barnett, *The Second Epistle to the Corinthians, The New International Commentary on the New Testament* (Grand Rapids: Eerdmans, 1992), 180.
2. John Piper, *Don't Waste Your Life* (Wheaton, IL: Crossway, 2005), 159.
3. John Piper, "He Will Send His Angels Before You," Sermon, Bethlehem Baptist Church, Minneapolis, MN, August 8, 1982.